The
Tap-Dancing
Lizard

The Tap-Dancing Lizard

337 Fanciful Charts for the Adventurous Knitter

THE TAP-DANCING LIZARD   50 stitches x 55 rows

by Catherine Cartwright-Jones and Roy Jones

 Interweave Press
Loveland, Colorado

For all the generations of ancestors
(yours and ours) who gave us the tools and skills
to make their visions into reality.

33 x 70

The charts in this book are accompanied by grid counts. The first number in each set is the width of the chart (number of stitches), and the second number is its height (number of rows). For example, the chart on this page is 33 stitches wide and 70 stitches high. When planning a garment, keep in mind that you will probably want extra stitches of background surrounding the design.

When you begin to work with a series of charts, we suggest that you take them to an enlarging photocopier and make copies at a larger size—preferably close to the stitch gauge you will be working at. Then you can position elements and design more easily.

Production by Marc McCoy Owens; cover design by Signorella Graphic Arts. Photos by Joe Coca.
Library of Congress Catalog Number 92-18569
ISBN 0-934026-78-5

Library of Congress Cataloging-in-Publication Data

Cartwright-Jones, Catherine, 1950–
    The Tap-Dancing Lizard : 337 fanciful charts for the adventurous
knitter / Catherine Cartwright-Jones, Roy Jones.
        p.   cm.
    Includes bibliographical references and index.
    ISBN 0-934026-78-5 (trade paper) : $16.95
    1. Knitting—Patterns. 2. Decoration and ornament—Animal forms.
I. Jones, Roy, 1949–   II. Title
TT820.C32   1992
746.9'2--dc20   92-18569

First printing: 7.5:1092:OB/CL
Second printing: 6M:492:OB

Contents

58 x 122

We've used this design, repeated over and over, in a twelve-foot–long scarf.

What's all this, then?

A friend of ours, while on a walking tour of Tibet, decided to commission a rug from a weaver in Lhasa for a friend. The weaver offered her an array of patterns to be woven into the rug, but he didn't say, "What patterns do you want?"; he asked, "How do you want your friend to be blessed?" That question speaks volumes about the purpose of decorative patterns in textiles, and about how much cultural meaning has been surrendered to factory-made fabrics.

Since neolithic times, patterns have been used to decorate textiles, primarily for magic, blessing, and protection, and only secondarily for beautification. All over the world, traditional clothing reflects the power of symbols. Women's clothing is adorned with fertility symbols, children's garments are decorated with charms for protection against disease, and the clothing of hunters and warriors is covered with symbols to inspire strength and courage. Regardless of your ancestry, you have a heritage of such symbols, and they can often tell you a great deal about your family history. Variations in a design motif can sometimes be traced to a specific region of a country, or even to a specific village.

The Industrial Revolution brought factory labor to the making of cloth, and later to the manufacture of garments. In recent years, home knitting and sewing have become less common. Individual craft and artistry in clothing have waned, and the sense that clothing connects its wearer to a larger community or a lasting tradition has disappeared in the industrialized world, except for the uniforms people wear as part of their profession or to signify their membership in an organization.

Though fashion has replaced meaning in clothing as distant factories have replaced local artisans, in some places patterns are still used as blessings, to be hand-worked with feeling. For modern city dwellers, knitted garments--especially sweaters--are among the few pieces regularly decorated with signs and symbols. Even some conservative dressers, who would never allow themselves to be seen in print shirts or blouses, wear elaborately patterned and brightly colored sweaters. Also, a sweater is one of the few pieces of clothing that most people seem proud to announce was made for them by a friend or relative, rather than purchased off the rack.

We began machine knitting sweaters for sale in the mid-1970s, because there seemed to be a demand for the old-style patterns that many people remembered but could not find in stores. When computer technology made it possible to design two-color patterns simply by drawing them on a grid and feeding it into the knitter, a whole new market of custom, one-of-a-kind knitting opened up for us, and that has been the mainstay of our business.

This is a book of charts for knitters. They represent years of looking at all kinds of clothing, art, pattern, and design books, and the daily effort of trying to find just the right design for a client. All the charts are on a rectangular knitting grid. They are useful for hand knitters, machine knitters, and duplicate stitchers. We have charted and knitted all of these at our studio for people who wanted something special to wear. Use these to knit blessings for your favorite people.

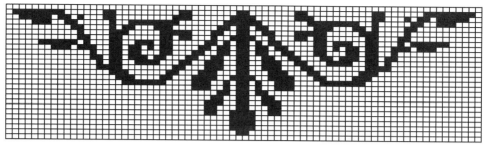

72 x 25

51 x 44

69 x 30

8

Introduction

Using the charts

For hand knitting

Find a simple sweater you have already knitted that looks as though you could lay one of these charts into it. Get out the instructions and compare the numbers of stitches and rows required for the sweater to the numbers of stitches and rows of the chart you want to knit. Will the design fit perfectly, or with only a little fiddling? Figure out the gauge you knitted in that sweater. Take your chart and a ruler to a self-service copy machine with a variable enlarging function. Enlarge the chart until the stitches in the chart match your knitting gauge. If the chart is large, you might need to enlarge it in pieces, and carefully trim and tape them together. (A 150-row chart at 5 rows per inch will be 30 inches long.) Pin your enlarged chart onto the existing sweater to imagine how the new sweater will look. Does it work? Start knitting the new sweater and work until it reaches the point where you pinned the bottom of the pattern on the old

sweater. Then begin to work your pattern into the new sweater.

We keep track of complex patterns in a simple way that works like a grid. It requires a collection of pull rings off of soda cans and a spool of brightly colored sewing thread. To start, find the middle stitch of your knitting and tie a bit of yarn there to mark it temporarily. As you knit the next row, slip a pull ring on your knitting needle every five stitches on either side of the center. When you reach the center, add a pull ring but also tie the yarn marker on the center pull ring to flag it.

Mark the center row on your chart with a colored marker; you can also draw darker lines across your chart to mark the five-stitch units and every fifth row. As you knit, count your stitches by the pull rings. Move the rings along with your stitches from needle to needle as you knit. Every fifth row, baste a brightly colored thread across the row so you can easily find your place in the chart. This is a

You won't get lost if you mark groups of five stitches and five rows. Use pull tabs from soda cans to mark the stitches, and brightly colored thread to mark the rows.

lot like cross-stitching onto canvas with guide lines.

Knit up to the top of the chart. Take out all the pull rings on the next row of knitting. Pull out all the basting thread row markers. Finish the new sweater as you did the original one.

As you practice this technique and become confident, you can look for more simple sweater patterns and plan other sweaters designed with the patterns of your choice.

For machine knitting

All these charts were originally knitted on a Knitking 910. They can be worked just as easily on a Knitking Compuknit 3 or 4, or the Brother 910, 930, 940, or 950. If your machine has a pattern width of less than sixty stitches, you can use the smaller patterns or you can set up a chart in front of you and hand pull the pattern.

If you have a very simple knitting machine that cannot knit two-color patterns at all, you can still duplicate stitch a chart onto a one-color sweater you have knitted, or you can machine knit the plain parts of the sweater and hand knit the patterned parts (at a carefully matched gauge). All of these charts have been used in garments of the type described in *The Prolific Knitting Machine*. If you have never drafted a sweater to knit on a knitting machine, that book may help you turn the charts in this book into a variety of special garments.

For duplicate stitch

Duplicate stitch is similar to cross-stitch, because you make a pattern by embroidering over a ground cloth, stitch for stitch. In duplicate stitch, each embroidery stitch exactly matches and lies over a knitted stitch. If you have a store-bought plain sweater, you can duplicate stitch one of these charts onto it. That will, of course, take the same sort of planning, centering, and counting as you would do for cross-stitch. Simple charts are easily done, and a small amount of duplicate stitch will make a mass-produced sweater unique and personal. Since it is difficult to fill a large area evenly with duplicate stitch, charts that have outlines work better than those with solid areas.

For the machine knitter, always hampered by the two-color-per-row limitation, duplicate stitch can be used to fill in the eyes of cats, dress up plain areas, and correct the inevitable pattern errors made by your computer.

Duplicate stitch

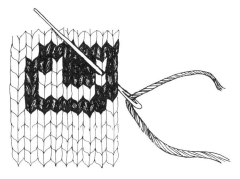

1. Bring the needle up from the underside of the fabric at the bottom of the stitch you want to cover.

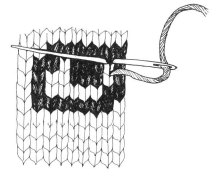

2. Following the V shape of the stitch, put the needle through the fabric at the top of the stitch. Duplicate stitch works best if the covering stitch follows the path of the base stitch, but does not split the yarn.

3. Completely cover the V of the stitch by inserting the needle again at the bottom.

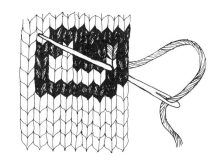

4. And so on. . . . If you are working on a large area, the stitches will go faster if you work from left to right, rather than up and down.

Materials and techniques

Fiber--and will it look good a year from now?

When you choose yarn for your projects, look back at the last many sweaters you have knitted and see what still looks good after several seasons. There are some knitted sweaters which looked like they *should* have been wonderful, but collapsed like a vampire in sunlight at the first laundering. Whatever yarn that was, avoid it. Good-quality wool lasts; money spent on wool is never wasted. Good wool doesn't sag and it keeps its color. Unlike Europeans and Canadians, Americans hesitate to wear wool. Good cotton is available, but it is not as durable as wool; it tends to sag and the colors may fade. It is easy to launder, but repeated trips through the washer and dryer can slowly beat it to a lump. Time spent on handmade things is precious. Use the best materials you can, so your hours are well spent.

Color theory, and the near infallibility of Mother Nature

There are no ugly birds. All flowers are beautiful. Animals always dress tastefully. If you are stuck for color ideas, go to a zoo and think of your sweater in terms of what the fauna are wearing this year, or go to a garden shop, where each flower is a fashion statement. The only difficulty you will have, when you have gathered ideas from those experts on beauty, is that yarn colors may not be as harmonious and subtle as nature makes them. If you still need color help, there are a few foolproof rules. Any two bright colors look good against black. Pastel colors look interesting on black. Dark shaded colors will sink into black. Any two bright colors look good against white. Dark colors look good against white; pastel colors tend to dissolve into white. A color against another color, unless you have seen the combination on an animal or a flower, might clash, so be careful.

Floats without drowning

If you knit in Fair Isle technique, you will have to cope with floats. If you are machine knitting, you can either avoid floats or tack them. If you want to avoid them, break up the design as much as possible so there are no floats more than two or three inches long. You'll see this approach applied in many of our charts. If, for the sake of the pattern, you can't break up the float (as in a large black cat), wait until the fabric is off the machine and then tack the floats down on the purl side of

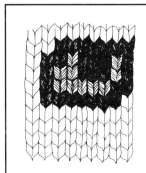

There! A green eye, duplicate-stitched for a cat.

Stitching down floats

The back side of this Fair Isle cat has long floats.

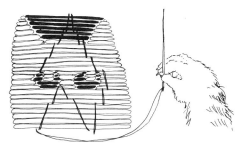

Make basting stitches, working so the thread doesn't show through on the front. All secure!

the knitting with needle and thread. If you are hand knitting, twist the yarn bobbins around each other between stitches as often as necessary to keep the floats under control--probably every inch or so. Some knitters twist after every stitch; this is especially useful for shawls, where floats on the back spoil the appearance, and for mittens, where floats catch fingers. Each twist will show slightly on the front side between the stitches. Check the results on a sample before making a decision about how often to twist the threads.

Fabric painting

Fabric painting is a useful way to add subtle color accents. For example, you can knit a calico cat in black and white, and paint in all the other colors.

Fabric paint is like acrylic paint, except that it "bites" into the fiber better. Deka makes a fabric paint that does not stiffen the yarn, is colorfast when washed or drycleaned, and sets permanently with a steam iron. Other good fabric paints are also available.

Fabric paint is different from dye. Dye spreads when it touches fiber, and paint stays put much better. You can use fabric paint as if it were watercolor. Mix your color on a white dinner plate with an oil painting brush, thin it with a little bit of water, and dab the thinned paint firmly into the yarn. Each stitch should be saturated with paint. If your yarn gets over-saturated, the color will run. Keep a roll of toilet paper handy so you can dab wet areas with wads of paper, so the colors stay put. When your painted area is dry, set the color by ironing. Specific instructions come with the paint.

Blot the paint to remove excess, and blot the edges of each painted area to keep the color from running.

Mix colors on a white plate.

FABRIC PAINT FABRIC PAINT FABRIC PAINT

ARTIST'S OIL PAINT BRUSH

A FIRM brush in this shape will push the fabric paint into the yarn.

For paler colors, thin fabric paint with clean water.

Adding color with fabric paint

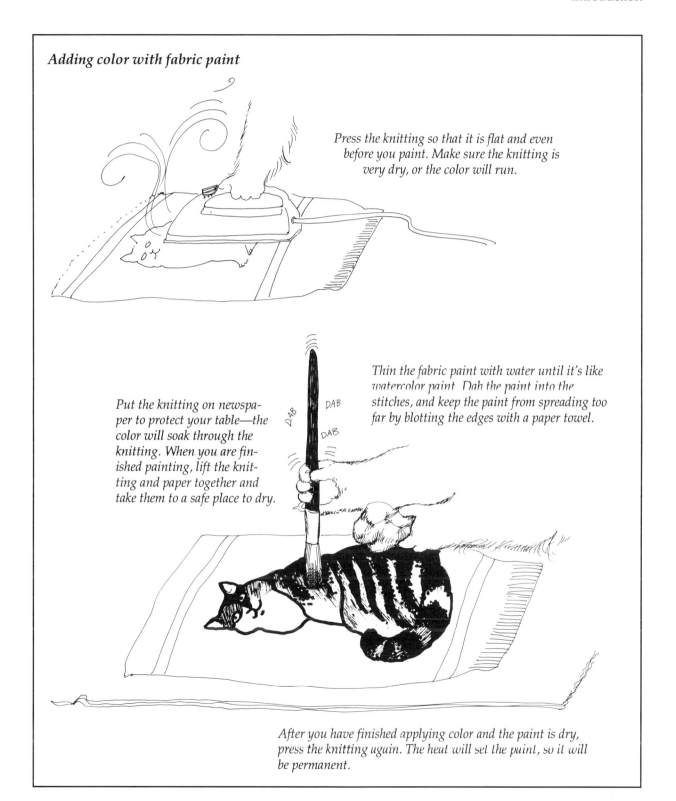

Press the knitting so that it is flat and even before you paint. Make sure the knitting is very dry, or the color will run.

Thin the fabric paint with water until it's like watercolor paint. Dab the paint into the stitches, and keep the paint from spreading too far by blotting the edges with a paper towel.

Put the knitting on newspaper to protect your table—the color will soak through the knitting. When you are finished painting, lift the knitting and paper together and take them to a safe place to dry.

After you have finished applying color and the paint is dry, press the knitting again. The heat will set the paint, so it will be permanent.

Embroidery

Embroidery stitches are valuable for adding color and texture to Fair Isle work. The stitches that work best are those that don't make the knitting puckery or inflexible. French knots of different sizes can be fruit on trees, accents on folk patterns, stamens on flowers, and grapes on vines. Crochet a yarn chain and couch it down (see the diagrams) to make a coiling vine, a collar on a cat, or a bow on a teddy bear. The crocheted chain will flex, and the texture complements the knitting. Crewel stitches make good flowers, and they move with your knitting and echo the stitch shape.

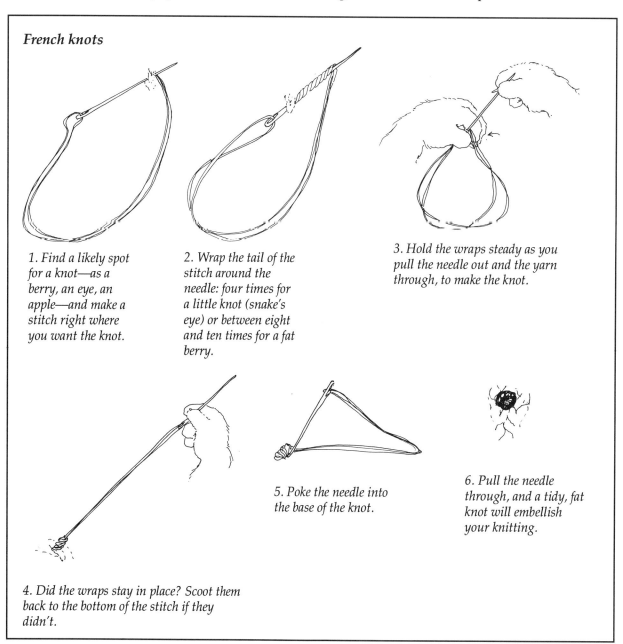

French knots

1. Find a likely spot for a knot—as a berry, an eye, an apple—and make a stitch right where you want the knot.

2. Wrap the tail of the stitch around the needle: four times for a little knot (snake's eye) or between eight and ten times for a fat berry.

3. Hold the wraps steady as you pull the needle out and the yarn through, to make the knot.

4. Did the wraps stay in place? Scoot them back to the bottom of the stitch if they didn't.

5. Poke the needle into the base of the knot.

6. Pull the needle through, and a tidy, fat knot will embellish your knitting.

Couching lines to add details

If you need to embroider
a line into your knitting
(cat whiskers, for instance),
use a couching stitch. . . .

For a thin line, like a whisker,

make the line with one yarn, and sew it down with the other.

For a thick line, like a grapevine,

make the line with a chain of crochet, and sew it down
with yarn of the same color.

I use a double strand of knitting yarn… it's simple and uses up scraps.

I use tapestry yarn doubled on wool knitting, or embroidery floss doubled on cotton knitting. There are so many colors!

Beading

Fair Isle patterns give you an outline for beading, and the fabric is firmer to work on than plain stockinette. Beading is tedious, but beaded knitting can be spectacular. Glass rocaille and bugle beads match the gauge of standard-bed machine knitting; larger beads can be appropriate for hand knitting. Beading adds a lot of weight; plan the placement of the beads so the garment won't sag. Try to keep the beading high on the sweater, and never work heavy beading along a hemline.

To outline a shape with beads (for instance, a dragon), string a long thread of beads, and couch the string onto the knitting; sew through three beads and couch to make a little knot, then sew through the next three beads. The work goes more quickly than if you sew the beads on individually, and it makes a smooth line. If one bead gets snagged when you are wearing your sweater, you will lose only those at that knot, not the five hundred others up the dragon's back. If you are stitching single beads, stitch through each one three times and make a tiny knot. Since you will want to wear your beautiful beaded sweater at every opportunity, stitch it carefully so it will stay beautiful for many wearings.

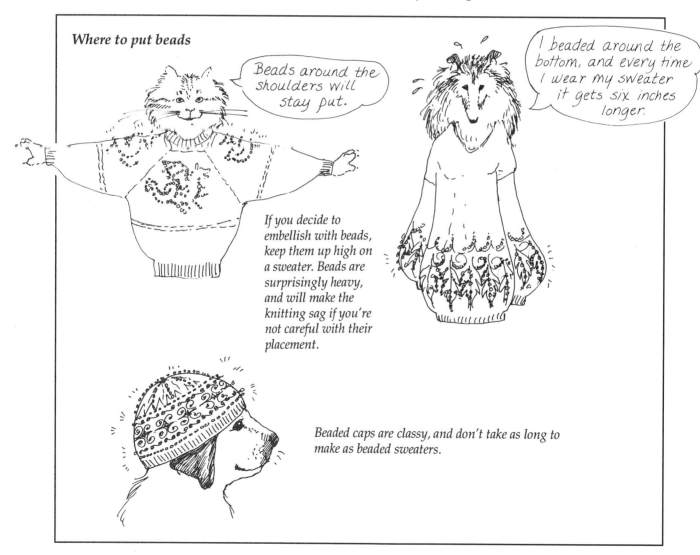

Where to put beads

Beads around the shoulders will stay put.

I beaded around the bottom, and every time I wear my sweater it gets six inches longer.

If you decide to embellish with beads, keep them up high on a sweater. Beads are surprisingly heavy, and will make the knitting sag if you're not careful with their placement.

Beaded caps are classy, and don't take as long to make as beaded sweaters.

Speedy beading

To add a smooth line of beads that won't fall off at the first snag—and to do it quickly . . .

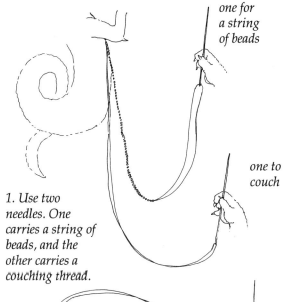

one for
a string
of beads

one to
couch

1. *Use two needles. One carries a string of beads, and the other carries a couching thread.*

2. *Slide out 1/3" of beads from the bead string. Scoot them into position. Stitch through the beads with the couching thread.*

4. *Couch the beads along the pattern, a few at a time.*

3. *Each time you have stitched through a small number of beads, make a stitch through your fabric which incorporates a little knot. If your beads ever get snagged, you'll lose only a few—not a handful.*

When the line of beads ends, slide the extra beads off the needle and knot both threads into the back of the knitting.

Regular thread
gets splitty ends.

Beading needles can be really hard to thread! If you use flat beading thread, you'll find it's easier to get it through the eye.

To make knitted foliage

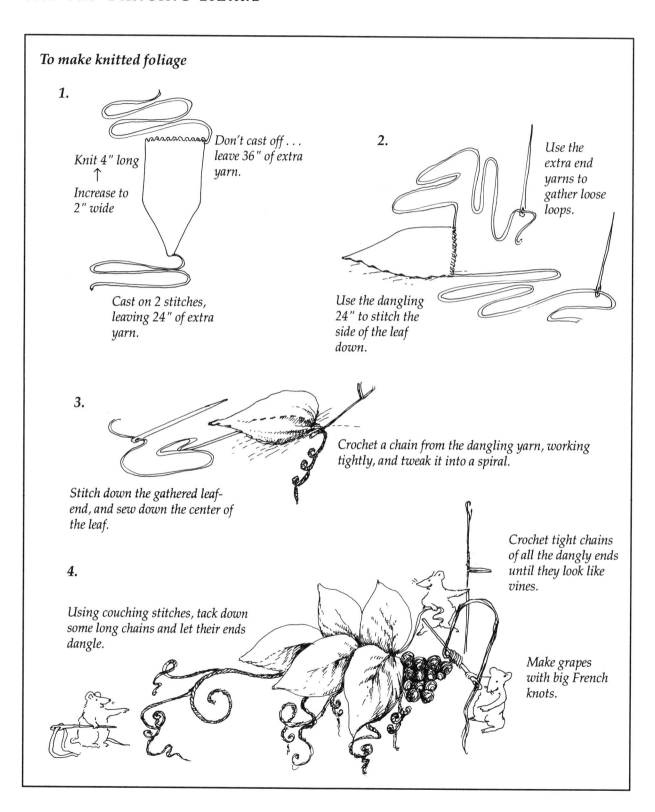

1.

Knit 4" long
↑
Increase to 2" wide

Don't cast off . . . leave 36" of extra yarn.

Cast on 2 stitches, leaving 24" of extra yarn.

2.

Use the extra end yarns to gather loose loops.

Use the dangling 24" to stitch the side of the leaf down.

3.

Stitch down the gathered leaf-end, and sew down the center of the leaf.

Crochet a chain from the dangling yarn, working tightly, and tweak it into a spiral.

4.

Using couching stitches, tack down some long chains and let their ends dangle.

Crochet tight chains of all the dangly ends until they look like vines.

Make grapes with big French knots.

Adding bits

Knitting machines allow you to make little bits of knitting quickly. Cast on two stitches, and increase on each side of every other row: you'll have a triangular bit in thirty rows and half a minute. Collect a basketful of these triangles in a few shades of green, and you can easily stitch them into a leafy vine on your knitting. Add clusters of purple French knots to make a grape arbor or lavender knots to make a flowering wisteria arbor.

Cast on two stitches, increase to 1½ inches, and knit along for two feet, then taper off, and you have the makings for a serpent to coil around your sweater. As you stitch your serpent into place, embroider eyes and a flickering tongue.

Knitted bits for appliqué will flex with the body of the sweater and will survive cleaning. If you try to add woven pieces of appliqué, the woven cloth and knitted cloth will never shift the same way and will tend to tear each other apart.

Supplementary serpents

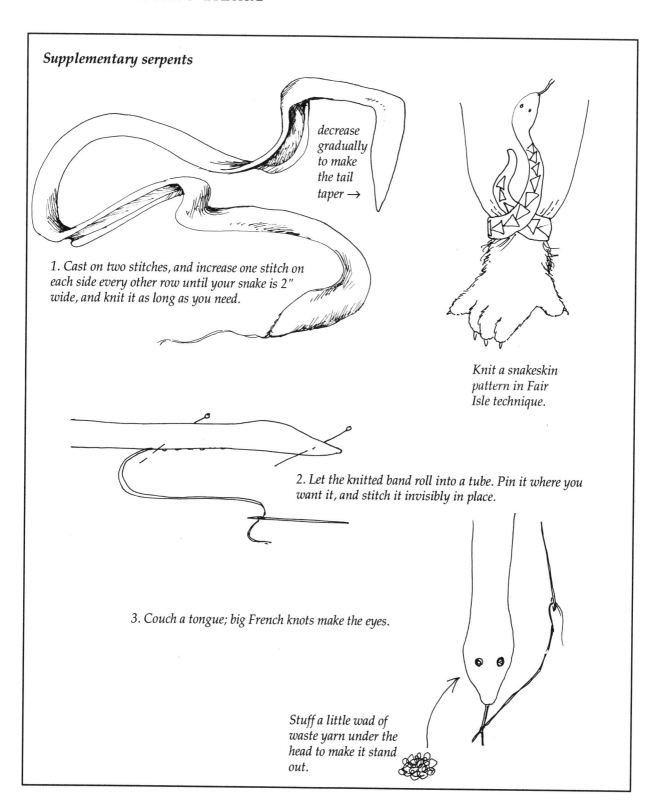

decrease gradually to make the tail taper →

1. Cast on two stitches, and increase one stitch on each side every other row until your snake is 2" wide, and knit it as long as you need.

Knit a snakeskin pattern in Fair Isle technique.

2. Let the knitted band roll into a tube. Pin it where you want it, and stitch it invisibly in place.

3. Couch a tongue; big French knots make the eyes.

Stuff a little wad of waste yarn under the head to make it stand out.

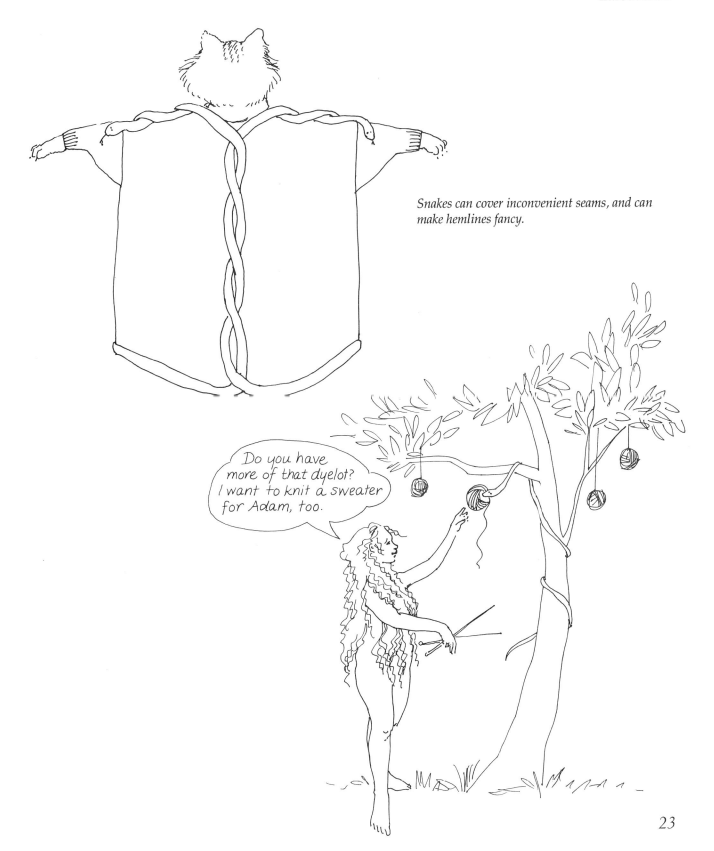

Snakes can cover inconvenient seams, and can make hemlines fancy.

Do you have more of that dyelot? I want to knit a sweater for Adam, too.

Foolproof sweater design

Here are some sweater layouts that have served almost infallibly for over two thousand sweaters.

Drop-shoulder sweaters

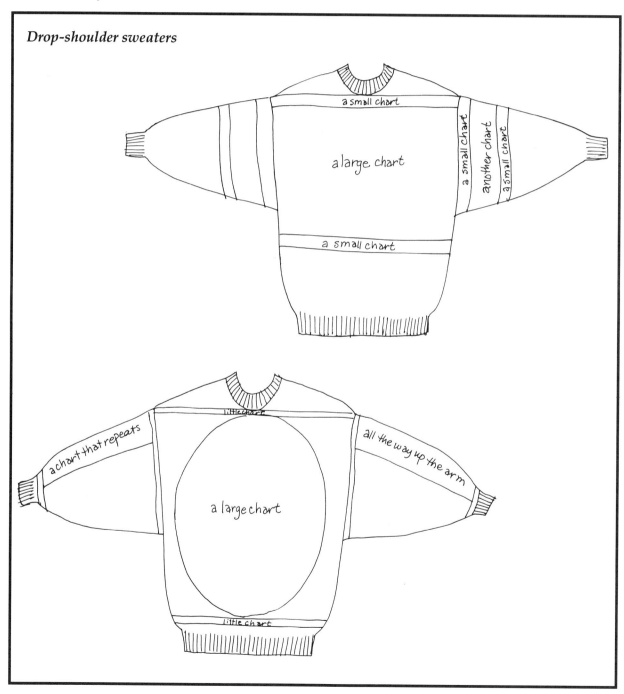

Two drop-shoulder sweaters,

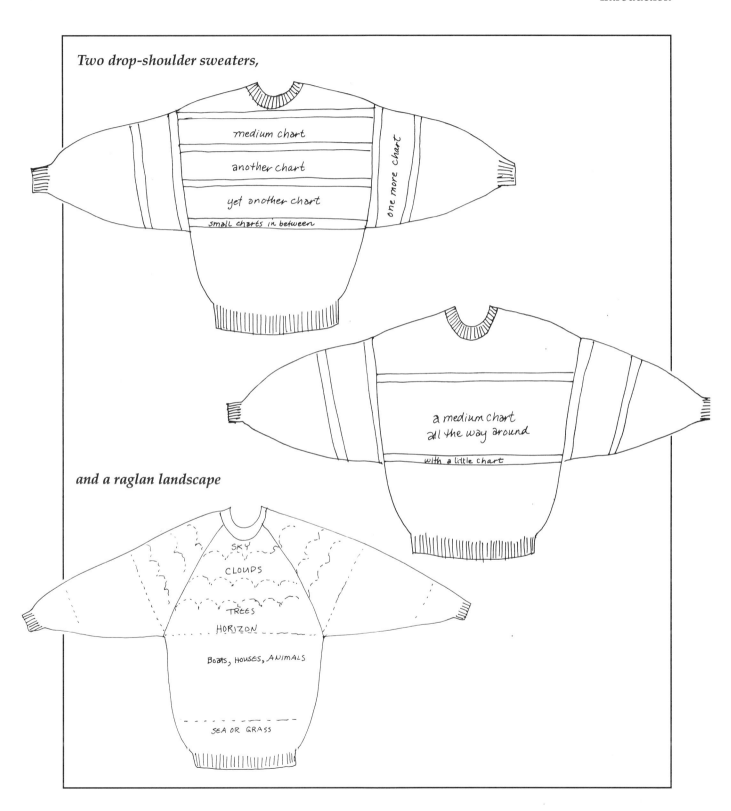

medium chart

another chart

yet another chart

small charts in between

one more chart

a medium chart
all the way around

with a little chart

and a raglan landscape

SKY

CLOUDS

TREES

HORIZON

BOATS, HOUSES, ANIMALS

SEA OR GRASS

Two coats

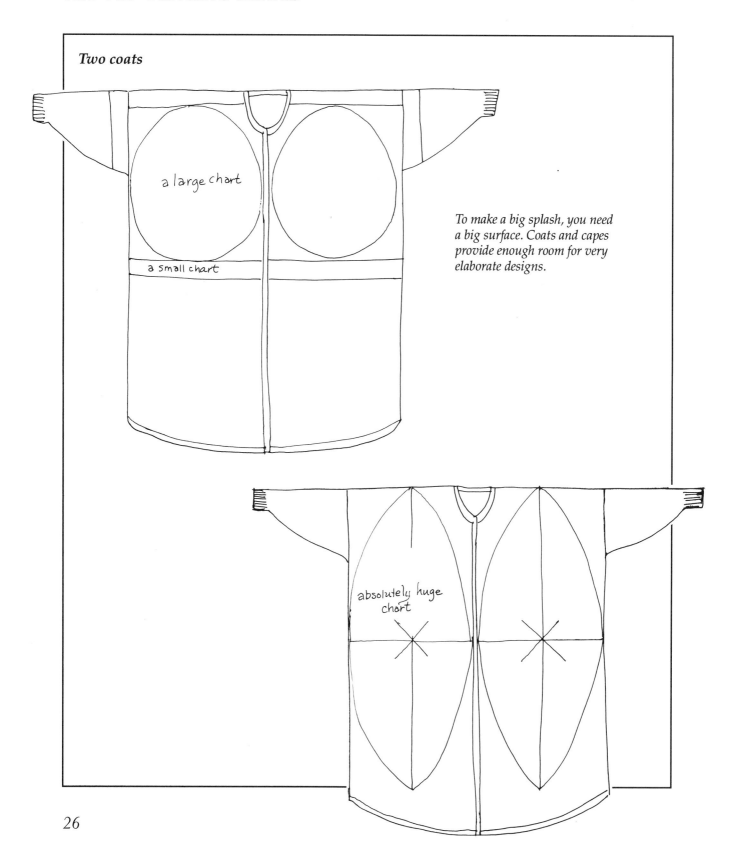

a large chart

a small chart

To make a big splash, you need a big surface. Coats and capes provide enough room for very elaborate designs.

absolutely huge chart

Past times and distant cultures

Adinkra

Adinkra is a West African cloth covered with patterns that bless, enlighten, and magically protect the wearer, or reveal some of his personality to those who know how to read the signs. Adinkra figures represent real or mythical objects or are symbols for traditional Ashanti proverbial wisdom.

Traditionally, these figures are printed in groups, within squares marked on big sheets of plain cotton cloth, or on long, narrow strips of cotton which are joined at the edges with multicolored embroidery to make the wrappers worn by Ashanti men. The designs knit well as horizontal Fair Isle bands by machine, or in blocks when worked by hand.

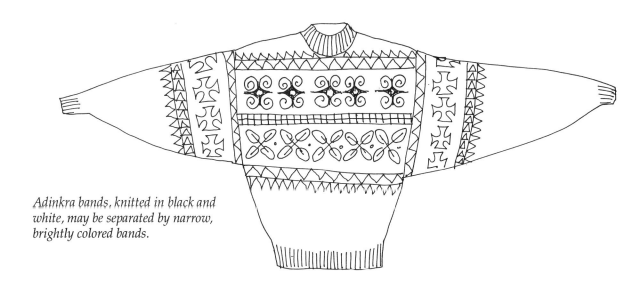

Adinkra bands, knitted in black and white, may be separated by narrow, brightly colored bands.

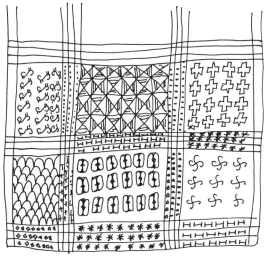

Adinkra cloth is white, stamped with black dye.

Adinkra stamps are carved from calabash (gourds).

Here are charts for some adinkra figures, along with their meanings:

← *Gwayu atiko:* "The back of Gwayu's head"; a chief cut his hair into this shape for a ceremony.
19 x 20

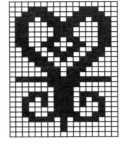

← *Sankofa:* "Turn back and fetch it."
15 x 25

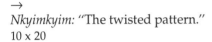

→ *Nkyimkyim:* "The twisted pattern."
10 x 20

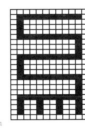

→ *Kuntinkantan:* "Do not boast or be arrogant."
21 x 21

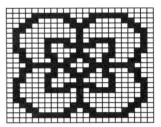

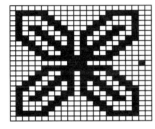

← *Nsirewa:* Cowrie shells.
20 x 21

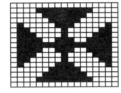

← *Musyidie:* Something to remove evil. A cloth stamped with this design was spread beneath the king's bed and every morning he put his left foot on it three times before he got up.
15 x 15

→ *Nkuruma kese:* Dried okra.
15 x 25

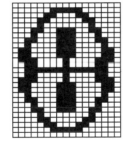

→ *Nsoroma:* "A child of the sky" or a star, from the saying, "Like the star, the child of the Supreme Being, I rest with God and do not depend upon myself."
15 x 15

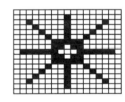

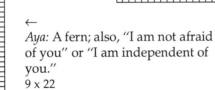

← *Aya:* A fern; also, "I am not afraid of you" or "I am independent of you."
9 x 22

← *Kwatakye atiko:* "At the back of Kwatakye's head"; the ceremonial haircut of a famous war captain.
23 x 15

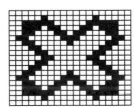

→ *Aban:* A two-storied house or castle, worn only by the king of Ashanti
17 x 17

→ *Ohene niwa:* "In the king's little eyes"; in the king's favor.
17 x 18

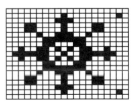

King's throne.
15 x 15

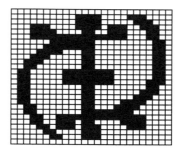

Gye nyame: "Except for God, I fear none."
23 x 25

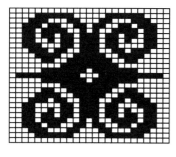

Dwemimi aben: Ram's horns.
23 x 25

Hye wo nhye: "He who would burn you, be not burned." This pattern was on the king's pillow.
9 x 20

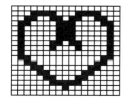

Sankofa: "Turn back and fetch it."
15 x 16

Nyame, biribi wo soro, ma no me ka me nsa: "O God, everything which is above, permit my hand to touch it." This pattern was stamped on paper and hung above the lintel of a door in the palace. The king would touch this lintel, then his forehead, then his breast, repeating these words three times.
11 x 15

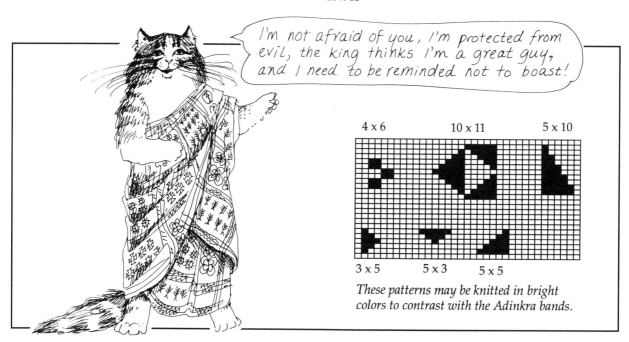

I'm not afraid of you, I'm protected from evil, the king thinks I'm a great guy, and I need to be reminded not to boast!

4 x 6   10 x 11   5 x 10

3 x 5   5 x 3   5 x 5

These patterns may be knitted in bright colors to contrast with the Adinkra bands.

30

Arslan Tash

Winged creatures with lions' bodies and nonlion heads were the guardians between reality and the supernatural in the ancient Near East. Kings commissioned statues and bas-reliefs of these mythical creatures to line the entryways to their palaces and temples; they aimed to impress their subjects and their enemies with their power and glory. These ram-headed sphinxes are from the ancient Assyrian palace of Arslan Tash. The use of rams', rather than eagles', heads is thought to indicate cultural exchange at that time between Assyria and Egypt, where ram-headed gods originated.

60 x 68

↑
center
stitch

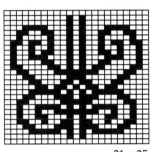

21 x 25

This is a tree-of-life variation . . . a stylized date palm.

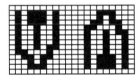

7 x 12   7 x 12

Here are upper and lower borders.

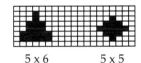

5 x 6   5 x 5

These are like old Assyrian polychrome brick patterns.

When used double, the center column of stitches occurs only once. The doubled pattern is 119 stitches x 68 rows. See top sweater on page 40.

Blackfoot

The Blackfoot are a Native American people who used to occupy the northern Great Plains. A Blackfoot man commissioned a sweater from us with his people's patterns, but his family had been separated from the land and the rest of his people for more than a generation. Old photographs of Blackfoot people (such as Curly Bear) and bits of Blackfoot clothing in history books provided these patterns for his sweater.

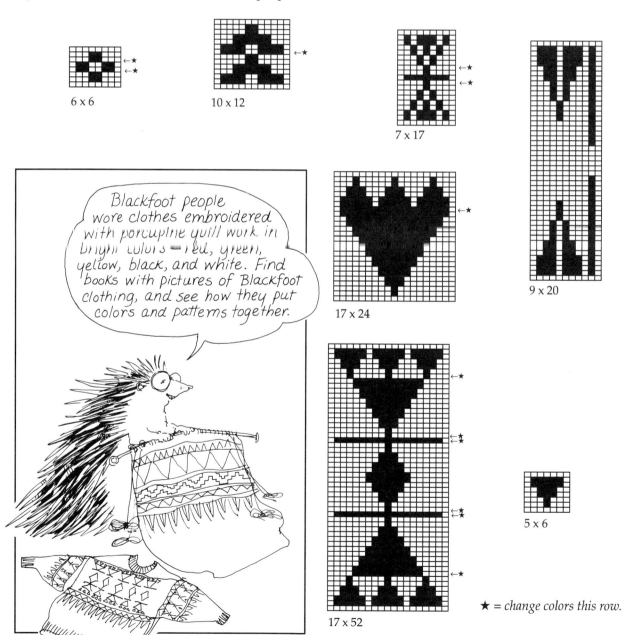

6 x 6

10 x 12

7 x 17

17 x 24

9 x 20

17 x 52

5 x 6

★ = change colors this row.

This calico cat sweater was knitted in warm orange and
black, then all the details were added with duplicate
stitch. The chart for the large cat is on page 103, and the
chart for the small cats on the sleeves is on page 108.

The sun charts on pages 142 and 143 provide the dominant designs in this cotton sweater, supplemented with geometric adinkra bands from page 30. Duplicate-stitched shading enhances the sun's image on the front of the sweater; an unembroidered version is on the back.

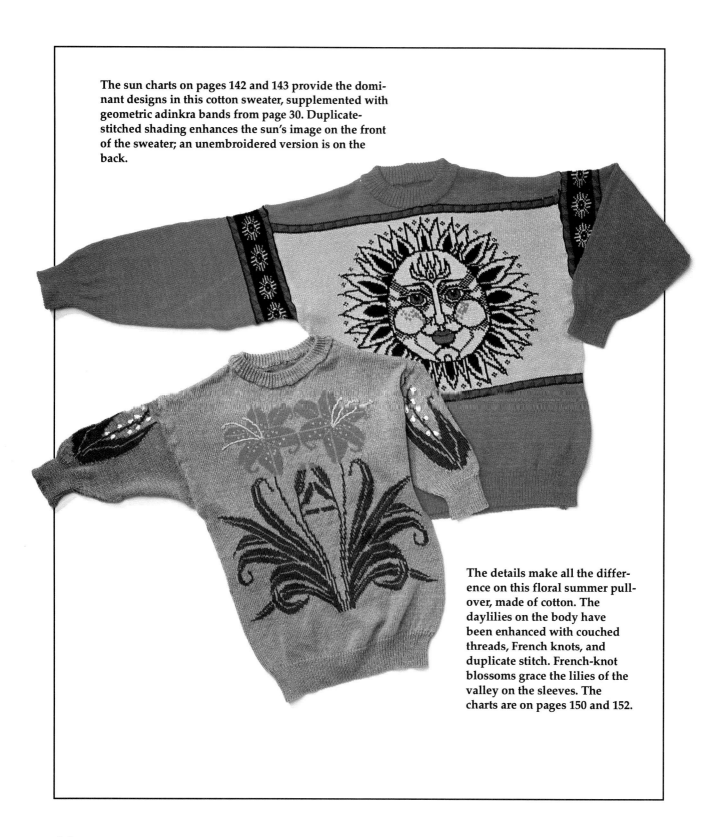

The details make all the difference on this floral summer pullover, made of cotton. The daylilies on the body have been enhanced with couched threads, French knots, and duplicate stitch. French-knot blossoms grace the lilies of the valley on the sleeves. The charts are on pages 150 and 152.

This seascape has different boat patterns on front, back, and each sleeve. The colors change gradually from deep water to shallower water, then to the sky and clouds. Lines of gulls were embroidered after the sweater was finished. The charts can be found on pages 133 and 134.

This dress shows one way to use the waterlily and the ripples beneath it (pages 153 and 154). Tiny beads have been sewn onto the water "dimples," to add sparkle.

The large rabbit and flowers for this sweater are on pages 127 and 128; the small rabbit on the sleeve hopped in from *The Prolific Knitting Machine,* page 194. The sleeve could carry more flowers instead . . . or a row of bright carrots.

Giraffes make a stately and unusual sweater, especially when combined with the bright colors of adinkra bands. The giraffes are on page 84, and the geometrics are on page 30.

These doberman pinschers were knitted in black and white, then colored with sepia fabric paint. The chart is on page 112.

Golden retriever puppies (page 113) are accompanied by dog bones and paw prints (page 111) in this wool pullover.

Large and small patterns can be used together, as in this light wool sweater, or to make coordinating sets of garments like those shown here. The elephants can be found on pages 80 and 81.

A small cap needs a small chart, filled with personality: the little dragon is from page 52.

Subtle variations in a basic plan produce two distinctive sweaters. Both pullovers feature the Islamic griffins from pages 57 and 58, with their coordinating charts. The griffins on the lower garment have been further colored with duplicate stitch.

Two wool pullovers and a cardigan based on historical figures. The top sweater derives its images from Assyrian sources, emphasizing Arslan Tash (page 31). The middle sweater shows ibexes, richly embroidered (page 61). The bottom sweater demonstrates the use of the French griffins (page 59); its sleeve chart is derived from the pomegranates in the corners of the main design.

Three more wool sweaters, simpler but no less inviting. On the top, dragons at the eclipse (page 51), with a simple sword design added to each sleeve. In the middle, a double-headed eagle (page 79), with a variety of intricate borders. On the bottom, two austere leopards (page 85), unembellished . . . and elegant.

Large buffalo in a wintry landscape decorate this warm wool pullover. Delicate colors produce a subtle effect; the charts are on page 76.

Deer combine well with a variety of settings. The main chart is on page 77. In this cardigan, the sleeves carry mistletoe (page 132), with embroidered berries.

Another cotton sweater, this one for a horse lover. The mare and foal on the body (page 123) are accompanied by a band of horseshoes (page 119). The horses on the sleeve come from a slight modification of the running horse on page 119.

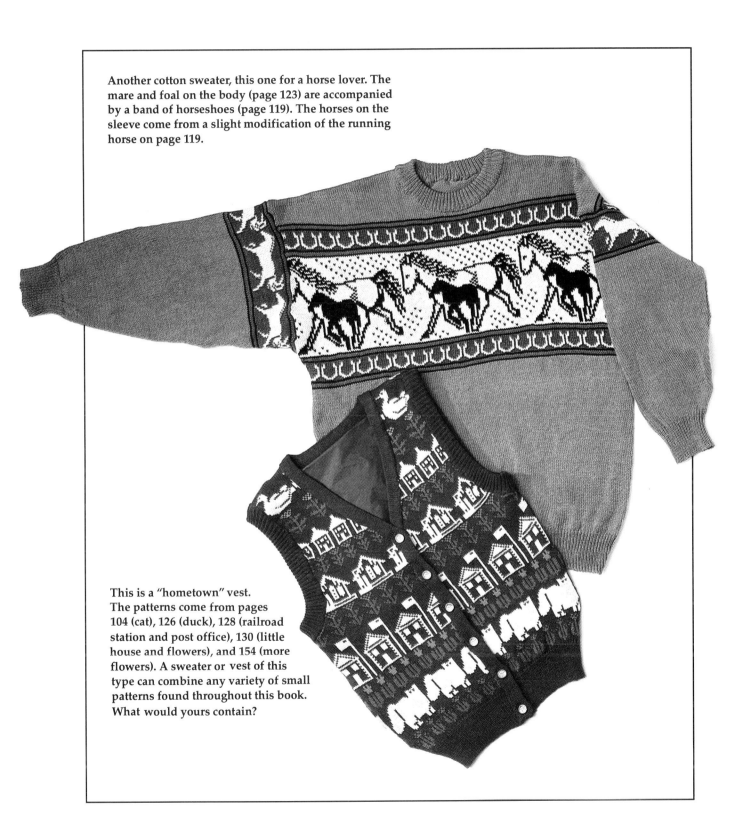

This is a "hometown" vest. The patterns come from pages 104 (cat), 126 (duck), 128 (railroad station and post office), 130 (little house and flowers), and 154 (more flowers). A sweater or vest of this type can combine any variety of small patterns found throughout this book. What would yours contain?

This long dress is mostly Pan and his jug (page 67), with grapes up the sleeves (page 68). The leaves, tendrils, and bunches of grapes on the shoulders were made with sculptural knitting and then appliquéd in place (techniques described on pages 20 and 21).

This is the back of a coat; the front has just as many dragons. After the fabric was knitted in deep blue and white cotton, intricate coloration was added with fabric paint. The charts are on pages 50 and 52.

One basic format: three distinct outcomes
for very different people. The happy cat's
chart is on page 98. The pug appears on
page 116, but is accompanied here by a
bone from page 111. The pandas and their
hearts come from page 90.

"Bicycat" (page 107) is for light-hearted souls who don't take them-selves (or their cats) too seriously. The cats on the sleeves (page 104) have bright, embroidered eyes. The hearts came from page 111.

Stockings and caps are quick to knit, and can reflect someone's favorite things. Basic stocking instructions start on page 157, and the Christmas charts are on pages 155 and 156.

Colleen's cap sports the cat you saw on the previous page, in a different context (charts on pages 104 and 111). The poodle comes from page 117, with bones from page 111.

Dragons

Chinese imperial dragon

The emperor of China was permitted to have a dragon with five claws. Lower-ranking folks got fewer-clawed dragons. Dragons in Asia are wonderful: full of great portent, blessings, and power.

Draco, the dragon constellation in the zodiac, rises each spring and brings rain. This chart is of the imperial sort of dragon. Chinese lore says that dragons could spit pearls. The circle he is coiling around is the Pearl of Wisdom. Here also are some Chinese characters for joy and blessings.

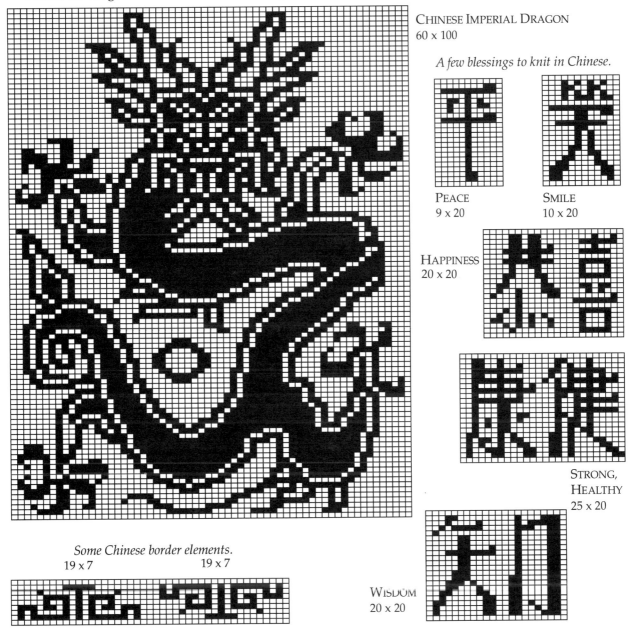

CHINESE IMPERIAL DRAGON
60 x 100

A few blessings to knit in Chinese.

PEACE
9 x 20

SMILE
10 x 20

HAPPINESS
20 x 20

STRONG,
HEALTHY
25 x 20

WISDOM
20 x 20

Some Chinese border elements.
19 x 7   19 x 7

European dragons

European dragons have a dreadful reputation. They sleep on heaps of stolen treasure, which are uncomfortable and put them in bad tempers. They have poor personal habits, venomous spittle, corrosive blood, and terrible breath. They ravage towns and disrupt the lives of fair maidens. Nonetheless, Westerners have always had a horrified fascination with dragons, and they are a popular symbol. They are appealing because they are not to be trifled with; many rulers may have felt that having a dragon as their symbol would awe the peasants and intimidate their adversaries. The Welsh have had a dragon as their emblem since Roman mercenaries from the Near East transported it to the British Isles on their banners. Others are fond of dragons for their subtle combination of mystery, romance, fantasy, and nastiness. For those who are Welsh, fond of legend, or find that the scaly fellows suit their disposition, here are dragons.

This is such a big pattern that it requires cape-size proportions on a standard-bed knitting machine. If you are clever about twining your floats as you hand knit, this could be a great shawl. At a gauge of five rows per inch, the pattern would be 60" long.
60 x 151

The full repeat format is shown on page 52, and a coat is in the photo on page 45.

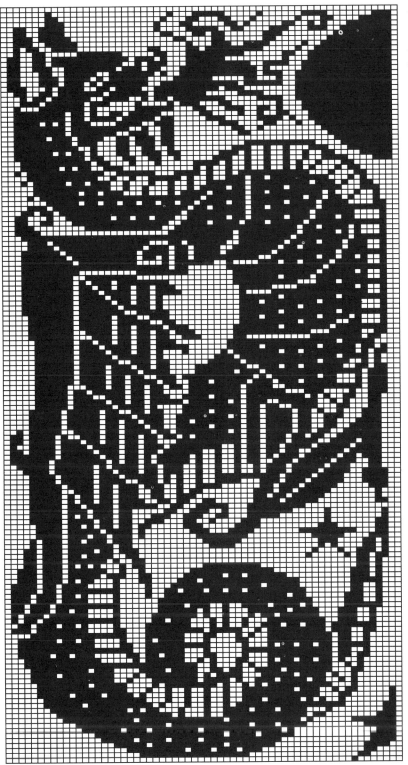

DRAGONS AT THE ECLIPSE
The doubled format is shown on page 53, and a sweater is at the top of page 41.
60 x 151

Pearl-finished round beads and silvery bugle beads bring sparkle to a dragon.

The pattern arrangement for a full cape (two repeats in each direction) measures 119 stitches x 301 rows.

Knit this in white on black for a great winter solstice cape . . . the moon at the center looks splendid when it is white . . . although this design has also turned out wonderfully in other combinations.

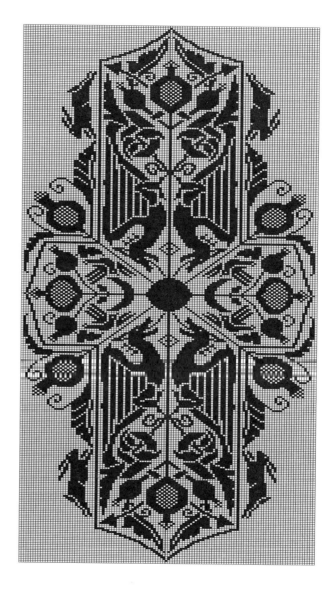

LITTLE DRAGON
55 x 30

A cap with this design is on page 39.

The doubled pattern measures 119 stitches x 151 rows.

This looks fabulous when the dragons are gold against a black sky, and all the dragons' scales are embellished with seed beads and pearls and rocaille beads. Then spark up the dragons' breath with red rocaille beads!

WELSH DRAGON
60 x 66

53

60 x 149

Feathered Serpent

The feathered serpent brought rain, fertility, and thunderstorms to Meso-Americans, and to southwestern and southeastern Native Americans, for centuries. The serpent goes by many names, and is today revered by those who still love the earth religion. The circle at the center is a medicine wheel. In many Native American traditions, a circle stands for the unity of all that exists. When divided into quarters, the circle

becomes the medicine wheel, a symbol that lies at the heart of their spiritual beliefs, because they see much of creation divided into groups of four: four cardinal directions, four kinds of animals (walkers, crawlers, fliers, and swimmers), four kinds of heavenly bodies (the sun, the moon, the stars, and the planets).

Along with the feathered serpents, this chart includes sky goddesses, lightning bolts, and the medicine wheel.

Repeated feathered serpent pattern for a cape; it measures 119 stitches x 297 rows. This is very easy to knit up on a standard-bed knitting machine that can handle a sixty-stitch pattern.

SKY GODDESS
*She goes with the feathered
serpent.*

*Knit the sky goddess in white, on a
black or midnight background.
Sparkle up her aura and the stars
by sewing on rocaille or tube beads,
as in the photo below.*
60 x 138

Griffins

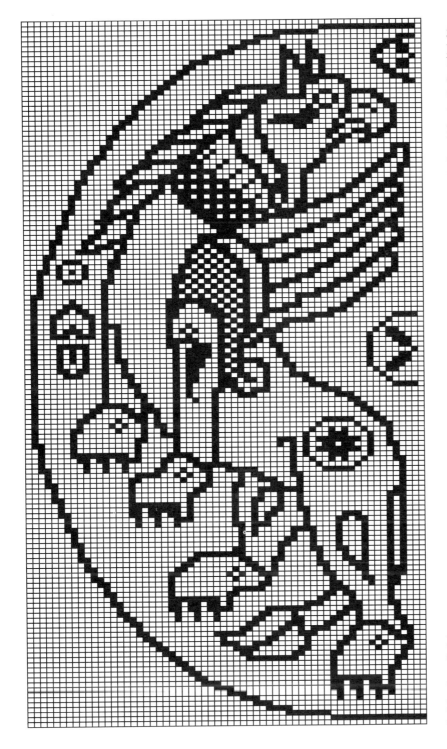

Half eagle and half lion, the griffin was the most frequently pictured guardian of the portals between heaven and earth in ancient Near Eastern art. Because the eagle was king of the air and the lion was king of beasts, a griffin, having attributes of both, was considered a great creature. When kings and countries adopted the griffin as their symbol, they were hoping to outdo their neighbors who had eagle or lion banners.

The griffins in the circle are derived from a medieval Islamic silk tapestry in which they were a part of a solar symbol. The other griffins come from a carved stone capital in a medieval French cathedral. The French griffins are surrounded by pomegranates, a symbol of fertility which probably came to Europe by way of the Holy Land, where, according to the Old Testament book of Kings, pomegranates were among the decorations on the pillars of Solomon's temple.

A pattern for borders.
11 x 11

ISLAMIC GRIFFIN
60 x 140

The doubled pattern is on the next page, and two sweaters are on page 39.

The Islamic griffins, doubled, measure 119 stitches x 140 rows.

The French griffins, doubled, measure 119 stitches x 150 rows.

Repeat this pattern vertically up a sleeve.
49 x 10

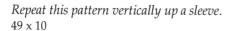

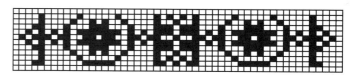

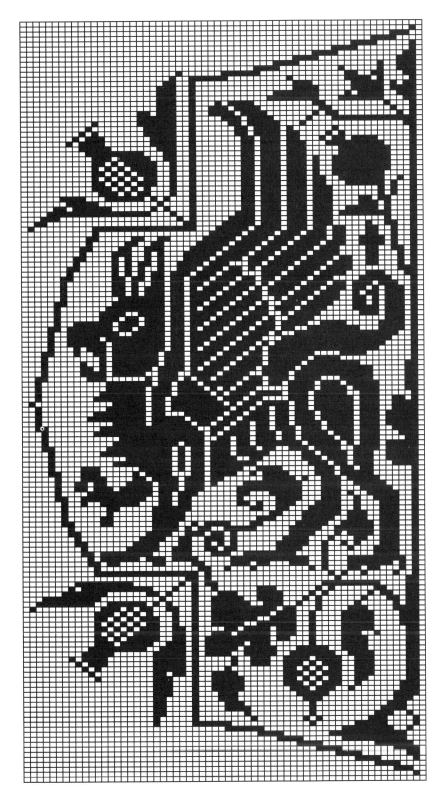

GRIFFINS FROM A FRENCH
CATHEDRAL.
60 x 150

*A sweater is shown at the bottom of
page 40.*

Hieroglyphs

These four lines come from the Egyptian Book of the Dead. The Book of the Dead was not dreary or terrifying for the ancient who recorded and used it; it was a handy guide and road map to the hereafter. Its author enjoyed life and wanted to make sure that anyone who had lived a kind, honest, and sincere life would have a comfortable afterlife, unhindered by uncertainties and stray demons. This passage is translated: "I have purified myself. I have become powerful. I have power over the steps of the shining ones." (We assume that means the person is of good moral and spiritual character and thus will not be troubled by bogeys.) Here are also a scarab, symbol of rebirth, and the Eye of Horus, the falcon-headed sun god. Horus' eye is a charm for safety and good health.

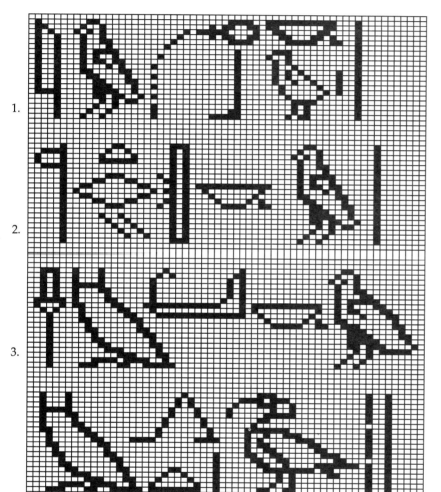

1. *"I have purified myself."* 51 x 20
2. *"I have become powerful."* 54 x 20
3. *"I have power over
   the steps of the shining ones."*
   60 x 20 and 55 x 20

UTCHAT
19 x 25

This is the Egyptian symbol for the sacred eye, sometimes called the Eye of Horus or Eye of Ra.

Border patterns for top and bottom.

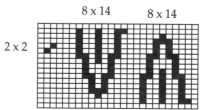

8 x 14   8 x 14

2 x 2

SCARAB
15 x 25

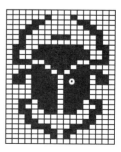

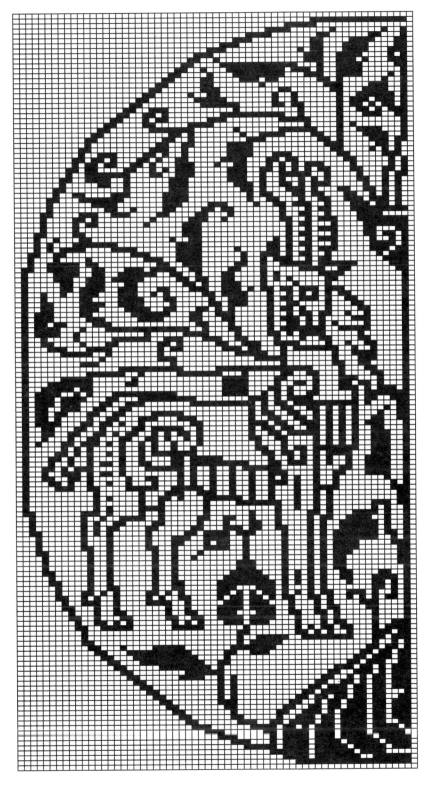

Ibexes

These ibexes, or wild goats, are from a tenth-century Persian silk tapestry. While Europe was trudging through the Middle Ages, Persia was enjoying a renaissance. Fine Persian textiles of this period were especially innovative and beautiful, and were popular with the wealthy and sophisticated aristocracy. The ibexes flank a tree of life and an oasis, a combination of images that goes back thousands of years in Middle Eastern art: cool water, a shady tree bearing fruit, and an elegant and edible beast.

IBEX
60 x 150

A sweater is shown in the middle of page 40.

*Doubled, the ibex pattern measures
119 stitches x 150 rows.*

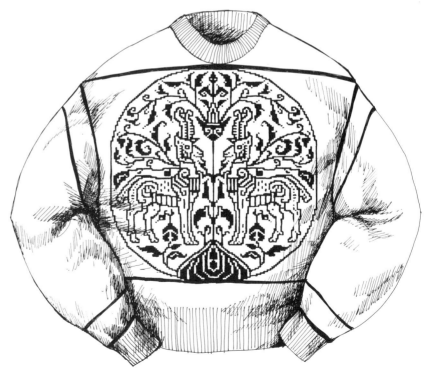

Lion Rampant

The lion runs rampant through heraldry, because it symbolizes strength and nobility, and the governing medieval classes fancied having that sort of reputation. The lion ruled over all beasts except those of the air, of whom the eagle was king. The Holy Roman Emperor took the arms of the eagle, and the unruly feudal lords were represented by lions. Lions are shown in more than four dozen poses in heraldry, all identified by French names, such as *couchant* (resting), *passant* (walking) and *dormant* (sleeping), but the most common is *rampant*, rearing with its forepaws in the air.

The lion looks most heraldic in gold on a deep red or blue background.
60 x 102

The Maya

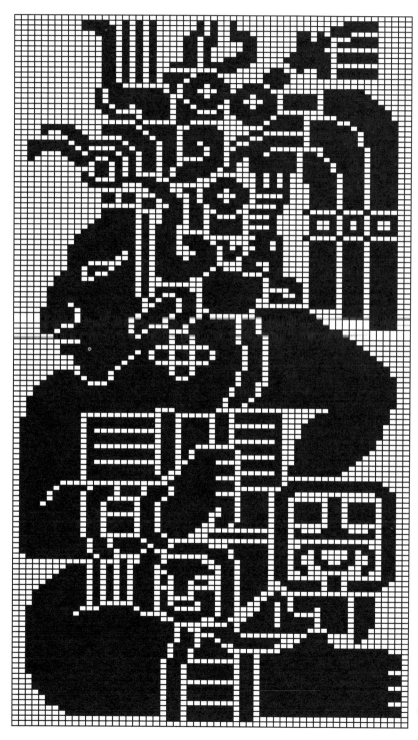

60 x 134

The gentleman in this chart was a dignitary in Copán, Honduras, in A.D. 700 to 800. His figure was carved into a jade plaque; his hand gesture suggests benediction. The Maya aristocracy were much concerned with perfection, elegance, intellectual and aesthetic refinement, and their own importance. The cross pattern is the cross of Quetzalcoatl, the deity of rain and eternal creation. The squared spiral is a frequent decorative element in Maya art.

MAYAN SCROLL FORM
12 x 11

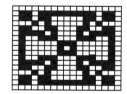

QUETZALCOATL CROSS
15 x 15

ITZCUINTLI
27 x 15

The animal figure is Itzcuintli, a kind of dog kept in pre-Columbian Meso-America; it was large, hairless, humpbacked, and reputed to be the ugliest dog ever bred. It must have been popular, though: it was as frequent a decoration then as cats are now in our culture.

The Maya dignitary knits up beautifully in Maya fresco colors: tan, redwood, sepia, ebony, jade, curry, cream, and Maya blue.

I am a Maya dignitary. I am an astronomer, mathematician, artist, architect, and urban planner — the cleverest fellow of the whole eighth century — and I have a great suntan and a wonderful hat.

I am Itzcuintli, a pre-Columbian stunningly ugly dog.

Pan and Company

Pan was an Arcadian shepherd-god who caught the imagination of ancient Greece. Half goat and half human, he represented the untamed nature of man, living in the woods and fields. Pan reveled in a bucolic life that intellectual, urbanized Greeks were giving up in favor of civilization. Pan was a pleasure-seeking, self-indulgent god, with no interest whatsoever in Greek mathematics, government, logic, or literature. The Christians objected to Pan's lustfulness and popularity and placed his horns and cloven hoofs on their devil. He was officially pronounced dead during the reign of Tiberius (42 B.C.–A.D. 14), according to Plutarch.

Nevertheless, Pan continues to be appreciated whenever people begin to feel overwhelmed by civilization. Shelley and Wilde held him dear, and Byron wrote a regretful ode on his passing. Painters have regularly invited him to accompany pulchritudinous ladies around bushes. Pan trots through Tom Robbins' *Jitterbug Perfume*, he is still sighted occasionally (most recently in Northern Scotland and in the canyons north of Malibu), and he is currently significant other to Gaia.

This chart is drawn from a bronze sculpture of Pan from the first century B.C. You will need to knit it in reverse colors: light pattern on a dark background. The green key border pattern complements it. Several grape patterns are also charted; they may be useful on sleeves.

Try augmenting the grapes on the large chart with a big French knot on each, and using lighter to darker shades of purple yarn to make three-dimensional clusters of grapes on the knitting. Then, with a lighter shade of green than that which you used to knit the leaves, add highlights in duplicate stitch to make the leaves look real. Sculptural knitting—embroidered and appliquéd grapes with tendrils and vines trailing over the shoulders and down the arms—makes Pan feel very much at home and results in a very theatrical sweater; see instructions on pages 16–17 and 20–23.

Dionysus and Pan became blended, though they were originally separate deities. Dionysus was a death-and-resurrection god, associated with wine and fertility; Pan was a woodland god. However, Dionysus and Pan were at all the same parties together, with feasting, wine, and romping nymphs, and identities got confused in the groggy mornings after. By the first century, no one seemed to know which was which, and they weren't sober enough to care.

Dionysus could shape-shift, sometimes into a panther. One of his Greco-Roman first-century devotees had a mosaic floor laid in his tomb depicting him riding on a panther, holding a thyrsus (scepter). This chart is drawn from that floor, though I made the rider a maenad (one of Dionysus' attendants), rather than a man. This chart should be knitted in reverse colors: light against dark. Like the Pan chart, it works well with grapes.

PAN
59 x 151
The doubled pattern appears on the next page, and a dress is shown on page 44.

Leaves for upper and lower borders.

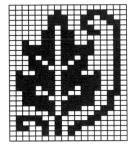

16 x 25

17 x 25

10 x 9

Pan, doubled, measures 117 stitches by 151 rows. Knit the Pan-and-jug pattern in white on a dark ground.

This repeats vertically up a sleeve.
50 x 31

33 x 26

Little grapes to repeat up a sleeve.
65 x 26 (doubled)

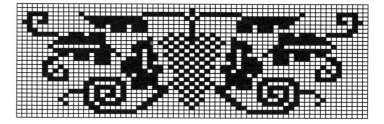

BIG GRAPES
77 x 90

These Greek patterns look great in Greek vase colors — black, cream, tan, rust, or wine... grape and vine colors.

MAENAD(S)
61 x 81

The doubled pattern measures
121 stitches by 81 rows. Knit
these ladies in white against a
dark ground.

Rain Bird

The Rain Bird is a beautiful and adaptable motif dating back to Zuñi pottery in the 1700s. The bird and feather forms were stretched by the Native American potter-artists into elaborate and elegant swirling or geometric patterns. Because they are creatures of the sky, birds are believed to be prayer-bearers. Crooks, drum beaters, bows, and feathers were included in the design because they were tools used to invoke rain. These charts are adapted from Rain Bird pottery designs.

RAIN BIRD
60 x 45

22 x 15

9 x 16   5 x 10

8 x 17   5 x 13

22 x 5

33 x 5

71

Unicorn

There probably were unicorns in times past, just as there are a few now. Goatherds knew that the horn buds on a newborn kid do not adhere to the skull in the first week or so after birth. They can be surgically shifted to the center of the forehead to grow together into one horn with little more veterinary skill than herders normally employ on their flocks. The resulting unigoat is a valuable protector of the flock, because its single horn is more dangerous than two conventional ones. If the technique of unicorn transformation had been kept secret, and rumors of miraculous cures due to unicorn intervention were deftly planted, the occasional unicorn would have kept a savvy goatherd bankrolled.

This unicorn chart is adapted from the fifteenth-century Siebmacher embroidery chart; my changes make it better suited to Fair Isle technique. Some flowers and fruits derived from medieval unicorn tapestries can fill out the knitting.

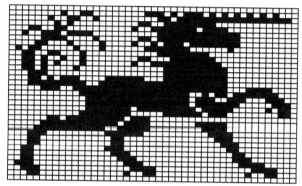

43 x 33

Unicorns look best knitted in white on a dark background.

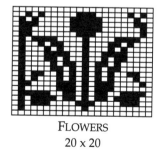

FLOWERS
20 x 20

CHAIN BORDER
6 x 4

STRAWBERRIES
16 x 21

Yoruba River Goddess

In Nigeria, the river goddess Oshun heals the sick and blesses people with children. The Oshun priestess is the mediator between the goddess, the river, and the people. This chart was adapted from one of the brass fans that is part of the Oshun priestess' regalia. The patterns are lizards and birds; the cross in the circle symbolizes the meeting of the powers of the spiritual and material worlds.

YORUBA RIVER GODDESS,
ORISA OSHUN
60 x 123
The doubled chart is on the next page.

Little coordinating charts.

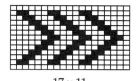

17 x 11

9 x 9

9 x 5

9 x 9

5 x 5

10 x 11

73

Doubled, the Yoruba river goddess chart measures 119 stitches x 123 rows.

In the wild

Buffalo

For the Sioux and the other peoples of the American plains, a buffalo hunt was something like a trip to the general store. The buffalo provided meat for food, hides for clothing and tents, and bones for tools and ornaments. The plains peoples believed that each animal had its own special magic or "medicine" and that humans could learn from observing and imitating the magic of the animals. The buffalo was such a good provider that it is no surprise that one of the characteristics of buffalo magic was a spirit of selfless generosity.

If you want a row of repeating buffalo, use the dots on the chart to catch up the floats that occur when carrying the yarn between animals. If you want to knit a lone buffalo on the prairie, leave out the dots. Here are some weary wintry weed charts, to go with snowdrift dots and some low hills and lowering blizzard clouds to make a late-February prairie buffalo scene.

BUFFALO
60 x 58

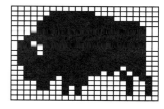

LITTLE BUFFALO
21 x 17

CLOUDS 30 x 20

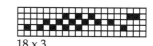

FAR HILLS
25 x 11

SNOWDRIFTS
23 x 4

19 x 5

18 x 3

NEAR HILLS
60 x 20

WINTER
WEEDS
9 x 18

Deer

In some Native American traditions, the deer is the symbol of love and gentleness that heals broken spirits. The deer's serenity and compassion make it possible for people to connect with the earth. The deer was a god in northern Europe during the Stone Age. Cernunnos was the antlered god of the Celts, who found enlightenment from contemplation in the woods. Neolithic cave paintings show shamans taking the form of deer. Around the world, legends about deer spirits center on the deer's solitude and gentleness. Knit deer sweaters for souls who like to be gentle and solitary.

DEER

59 x 140

If you knit this in brown on white, stitch the nose and eyes in black . . . otherwise, knit the deer in black on tan. See the oak leaves (page 131) for an ideal companion pattern; for a knitted example with mistletoe, see page 42.

Eagle

The essential eagle

The eagle was the symbol of the western Roman Empire. When Charlemagne became Emperor of the West in A.D. 800, he put an imperial eagle on his palace to establish his political legitimacy. Eagles on state crests have moved all over the world by marriage and alliance, and they turn up over government offices, on money, and on coats of arms.

Eagles represent glory and power, because they are beautiful and powerful in flight, and can have almost any small to medium animal for lunch. If you knit this eagle as a white bird on a red ground, it becomes the Polish emblem and will be much appreciated by your Polish friends.

The double-headed eagle

When the old Roman Empire broke in two, the double-headed eagle became the symbol of the eastern Empire. As political power shifted around through marriage, conquest, and alliance, the double-headed eagle moved into the crests of countries, families, and towns. The czars used it as their symbol, and their allies borrowed it. Those who used the two heads claimed that this version was the emperor's eagle, and that the single-headed eagle represented only the Roman king and was thus inferior. When Napoleon borrowed the double-headed eagle, it became less popular in Eastern Europe for awhile. This chart makes a lovely sweater for someone of Russian or Austrian ancestry or for someone who has an imperial personality.

To make this eagle Polish, knit it as a white bird on a red ground.
50 x 110

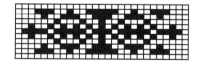

This is a pattern to repeat vertically up a sleeve.
25 x 9

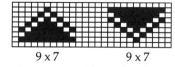

9 x 7   9 x 7
An upper and lower border.

RUSSIAN DOUBLE-HEADED EAGLE
A pullover with this design is on page 41.
60 x 95

11 x 11

8 x 12

8 x 12

Edge patterns

The doubled Russian eagle measures 119 stitches x 95 rows.

Elephants

Elephant herds are companionable matriarchal groups. When the members are separated even for a short while, they become very excited when they get back together, trumpeting and whirling about to greet each other. The ladies have two-year pregnancies and are tender mothers. When they need a gentleman companion, they sing infrasonic songs that can be heard over great distances by solitary waiting males. Elephants are immense, ancient, intelligent, and familial. We need more of them.

These designs are shown in a cap, sweater, and scarf set on page 38.

60 x 94

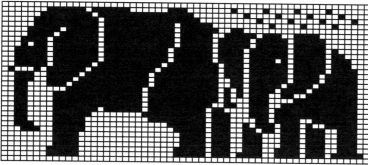

56 x 30

*This is how the elephant patterns work in a repeating arrangement;
the large elephant overlaps one column in the repeats.*

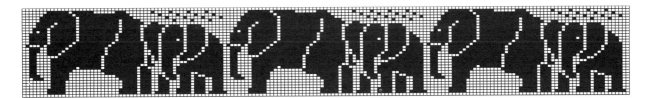

Fish

Largemouth bass burst from weedy depths and thrash furiously and magnificently against the lure. A bass arching into the air thrills the hearts of some fishermen. Other fishermen just let the bass muck about in the weeds. They visit lakes because bass neighborhoods do not include phones, traffic, and impatient boors. For bass appreciators, here are two largemouth bass charts. The dots are meant to look like ripply, bubbly water, and they catch up the long floats formed when knitting three fish repeated across the sweater. If you're knitting just the one bass, omit the bubbles.

Here also are small patterns of perch, catfish, stickleback, and a pike, which also live in peaceful neighborhoods.

LARGER-MOUTH BASS.
Knit the big fish in dark, fish colors on a pale or white watery-colored background.
61 x 117

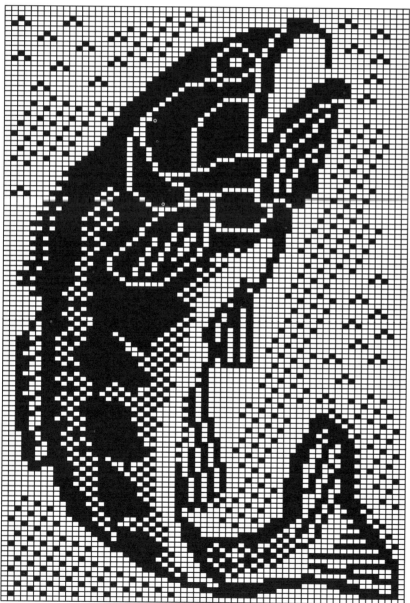

STICKLEBACK
24 x 13

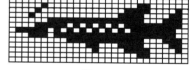

PIKE
26 x 11

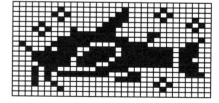

CATFISH
29 x 17

LARGEMOUTH BASS
60 x 80

Knit the little fish in pale, fishy colors against a dark, watery-colored background.

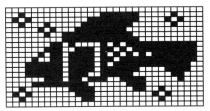

PERCH
29 x 18

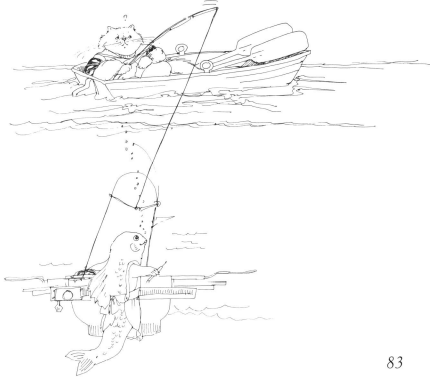

Giraffes

The giraffe nibbles acacia leaves and watches the movement of lions far away. She doesn't worry about anything leaping on her suddenly because she can see everything for a long distance. Her height is enough to intimidate most nearby animals, and the rest she can run from. The giraffe is a model of self-composure. People with an atmospheric dignity or those whose feet are simply a great distance from their shoulders seem very fond of giraffes.

Three giraffes parade across a pull-over on page 36.

60 x 132

Leopards

Knit these leopards in white against a black ground; they seem to be guarding something in the darkness, or perhaps they pose impossible riddles to pass-ersby. If you answer their rid-dles, do they vanish in a puff of smoke, or do they give you a clue to treasures hidden beyond the mountain and accompany you partway?

The doubled pattern appears on the next page, and a sweater is on the bottom of page 41.

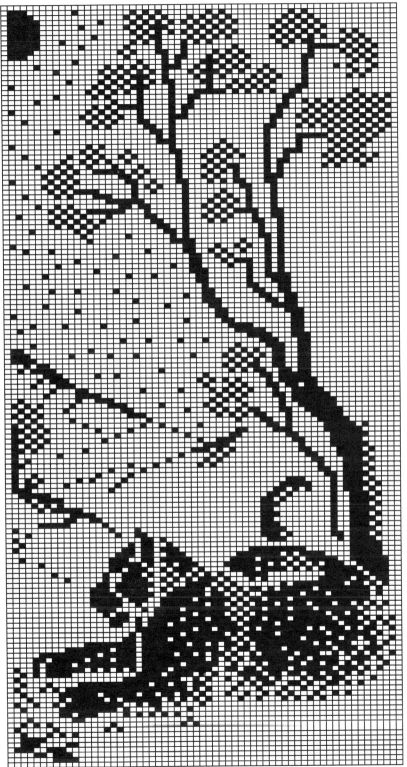

60 x 151

Knit this landscape in white on black. For a spectacular sweater, sew silvered rocaille beads onto the stars and moon, and add gold beads to highlight the leopards. The doubled leopards measure 119 stitches x 151 rows.

Lizards

In some Native American traditions, lizard represents dreaming. Lizard sits with his eyes half closed, looking into shadows to see the future, fears, or hopes; lizard knows it's important to pay attention to dreams.* Here are some dreaming lizards.

*Sams and Carson, *Medicine Cards*, pages 181–83.

Knit this wild lizard in a brilliant color against black, then duplicate-stitch the white of the eyes. The sides of the lizard below are embroidered for more texture.
60 x 95

Here are some small patterns, like lizard markings, for border bands.

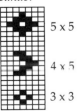

5 x 5

4 x 5

3 x 3

CHAMELEON
39 x 22

87

Knit this fellow in a lizardly color against a black background.
60 x 77

Ocelot

Ocelotl is a Nahuatl word meaning jaguar, an animal the ancient peoples of Meso-America found fascinating. The jaguar was a skillful predator (occasionally of people), and was symbolic of earth and darkness. Ocelot and jaguar priests and knights had ritual battles with the eagle priests and knights, who symbolized sky and light. For those who admire stealth, grace, and pouncing in the dark, here is an ocelot.

60 x 71

Owls

The owl was a symbol of Athena. The larger chart is from a silver tetradrachm from fourth-century–B.C. Athens, and shows Athena's name and her owl. Athena was the owl-eyed maiden goddess, and she is sometimes depicted carrying a little owl on her shoulder. Though Athena was the goddess of wisdom, and "wise old owl" is still in the language today, *real* owls are neither tractable nor teachable. Throughout the Middle Ages, they accompanied seers and alchemists, but they have only solemn great eyes and nothing magical between the ear tufts. They are also disinclined to shape-shift with witches, but they are beautiful to watch, lovely to listen to in the night, and dandy as mousetraps around the barn.

ATHENA'S OWL
59 x 78

10 x 9

LITTLE OWL
15 x 25

LITTLE OWL
AND THE MOON
22 x 32

Pandas

The panda is an admirable creature: solitary, quiet, prone to gracious rotundity, and solicitous as a mother. There aren't enough pandas.

If you knit the panda in Fair Isle technique on a knitting machine, you'll need to stitch down the floats on the panda mama's back. There's a panda scarf on page 46.

60 x 85

A Chinese figure to border the panda.
10 x 9

Another obvious border.
5 x 5

Penguins

A penguin swoops and glides under water, gobbling squid and small fish, and dodging ravenous seals, then trudges gracelessly back up the ice shelf to its colony of identical neighbors, carefully locates its rock, and waits in the cold for the next antarctic tide. Here are some charts, for use by residents of snowbelt cities who might feel like penguins as they trudge grimly from subway to suburb in February.

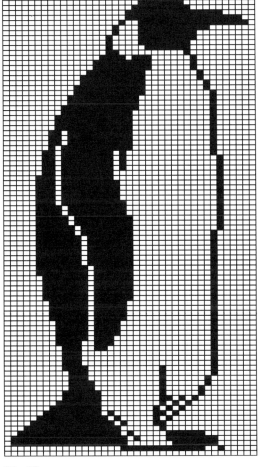

37 x 90

15 x 30

Peregrine Falcons

The peregrine does lunch in midair. It flies high above its prey, preferably another bird, then plummets down with wings partially folded, extends its claws, and hits the prey like a missile. Many poets, philosophers, and falconers have made much of the peregrine's habits: the female is larger and more aggressive than the male. Peregrines have a keen sense of strategy in their hunting, often stooping (attacking from above) out of the sun or from behind cliffs. Though peregrines were devastated by pesticides, their numbers are increasing, with determined efforts from peregrine appreciators, and some individuals now thrive in city-canyons, where they attack pigeons from their nests atop urban high-rises.

60 x 69

This falcon is stooping.
11 x 15

This border pattern is a talon. . . .
5 x 10

This bird's pattern overlaps one column in the repeat, like this:

Snakes

No folk tradition regards snakes as ordinary. In Indo-European and Native American legends, venomous snakes appear as symbols of healing, the antithesis of their poisonous bites. The Hopi believe that the jagged tracks some rattlesnakes leave in the desert sand identify them as sacred to the thunder god, and they use the snakes as messengers in their rain rituals. Other Native Americans wove stories of the snakes' "rebirth" through the shedding of their skins. Adolescents seem fond of snakes just because they make their mothers flinch.

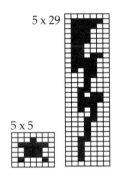

5 x 29

5 x 5

59 x 85

36 x 30

I made my serpent fly in the night with rainbows and lightning!

Wolves

To the Native Americans, the wolf is the pathfinder, the teacher who brings in new ideas. The wolf's ally is the moon, and he bays at the moon to connect with the new ideas in the subconscious.* Here is a wolf baying at the moon on a starry night.

---

*Sams and Carson, *Medicine Cards,* page 97.

5 x 10

60 x 90

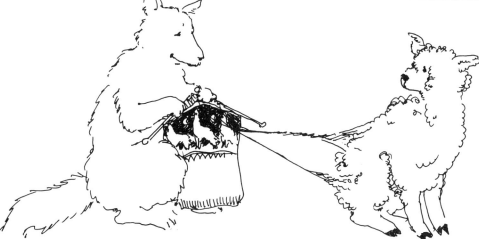

94

Not-so-wild

Cats

The worship of cats began in Egypt; the Egyptians took their cats very seriously and condemned to death anyone who killed a cat. Bast was the cat-mother goddess, and her festivals were full of music, dance, and sexual cavorting (like your housecat). Cat worship continues today, less formally, on sofas in comfy houses.

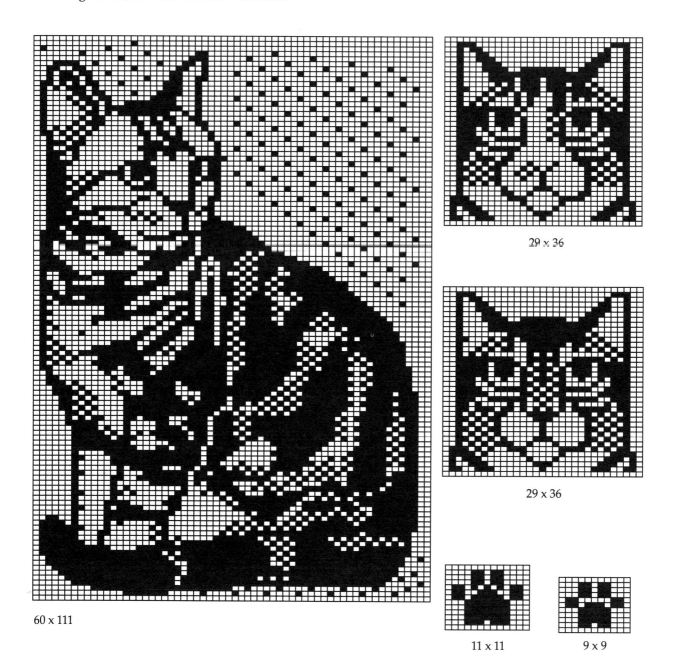

29 x 36

29 x 36

60 x 111

11 x 11

9 x 9

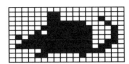

16 x 10

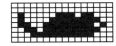

14 x 5

Little cat bits; use in rows, or for hand knitting.

15 x 5

24 x 5

45 x 73

19 x 5

20 x 5

This cat is a good one to work entirely in duplicate stitch on a plain-colored stockinette ground.
60 x 68

Two happy cats, well suited to intarsia technique on a machine, or to hand knitting. The cat on the left frolics on a scarf, page 46.
58 x 135

60 x 149

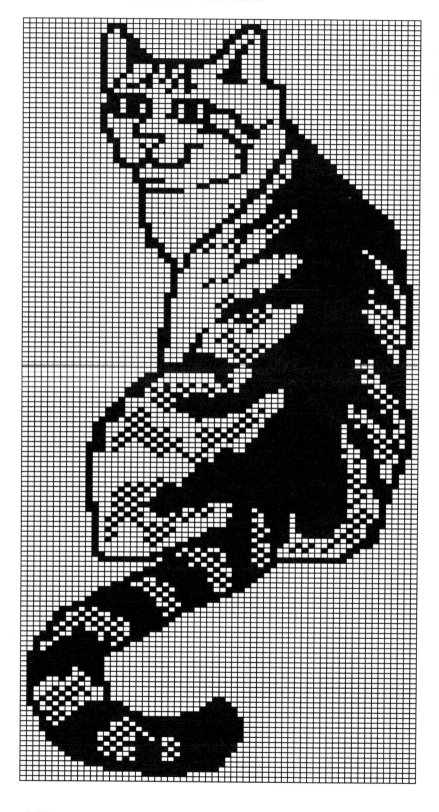

Try using duplicate stitch to add a pink nose and green eyes. Then stitch in a ribbon with a bow around the cat's neck.
60 x 151

Knit this cat in gray or black on white, with duplicate stitch to brighten the eyes.
60 x 134

Do you have a calico cat like this? Try knitting her in black on copper; then duplicate-stitch her white muzzle and vest, her gold eyes, and the tan and gray bits.
60 x 128.
See the color photo on page 33.

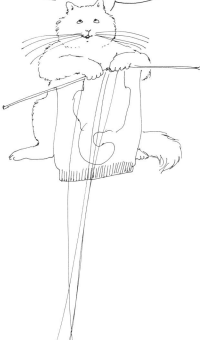

Some people do crossword puzzles in ink to relax. I love to knit complex patterns! I let my life go on hold for a few rows — and purl my problems away!

TUMBLING CATS
For a cape.

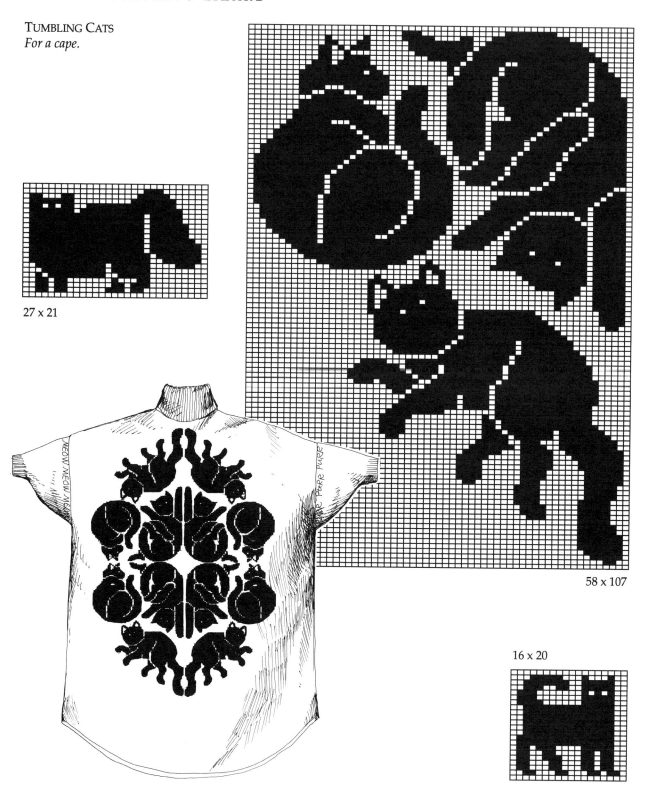

27 x 21

58 x 107

16 x 20

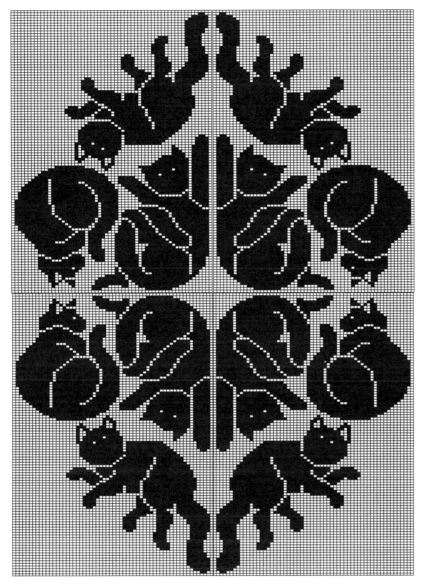

The full set of cats needs some rows of "background" stitches between the mirrored repeats. With two "blank" rows, the full repeat in both directions measures 118 stitches x 216 rows.

18 x 31

28 x 26

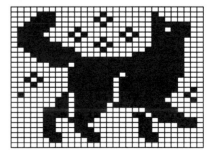

22 x 18

Here are two very silly cats, best
suited for a standard-bed knitting
machine, Fair Isle technique, or
double-bed knitting.
60 x 142

See this cat on a pullover on page 47.

61 x 116

On this cat, I use duplicate stitch to add golden eyes.

29 x 38

61 x 98

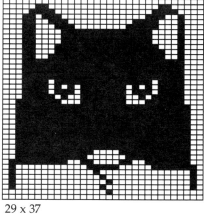

29 x 37

This is a nice pattern to repeat vertically up a sleeve. You can see it in use on page 33.

55 x 38

The pattern on the right makes a great cardigan, with two cats facing each other across the buttons. 60 x 94

28 x 39

29 x 40

This kitty looks nice in gray heather yarn on white, with the eyes colored in duplicate stitch. 58 x 55

If you knit several cats across a sweater in Fair Isle technique, use background dots to pick up the floats. Otherwise, ignore the background dots.
60 x 125

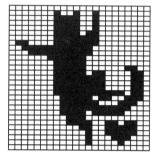

20 x 27

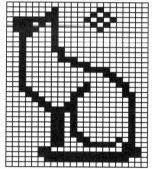

20 x 31

28 x 39

Dogs

Your dog is the one creature who is *always* glad to see you coming. Your dog adores you, listens to you, respects you, comes when you call, protects you, and will forgive you anything. Dogs probably were not made gods, as cats were, because they are so willing to grovel. They have, though, been on laps of kings, queens, and several gods. Here are charts of some good doggies.

ROTTWEILER
Because of long floats, this pattern is best worked by hand with intarsia, or on a double-bed machine.
60 x 133

Here are some essential little bits.

10 x 5   5 x 5

19 x 5

9 x 10

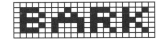

20 x 5

GOLDEN RETRIEVER
60 x 60

Knit in pale gold on a black background.

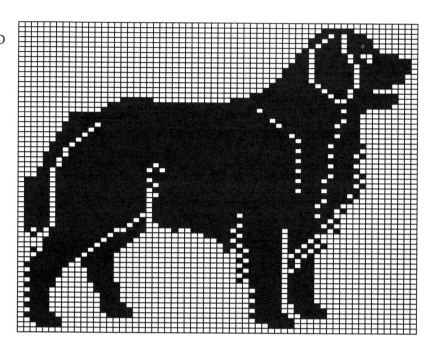

DOBERMAN PINSCHER
60 x 94

If you are hand knitting, work the dobie's muzzle and markings in tan; if you are machine knitting, color in the markings with sepia-colored fabric paint. For an example, see the vest on page 37.

29 x 27

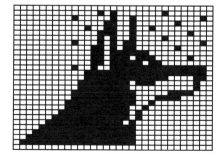

GOLDEN RETRIEVER
50 x 120

This is a cuddly golden retriever puppy, if you knit it in sand on black. There's a puppy sweater on page 37.

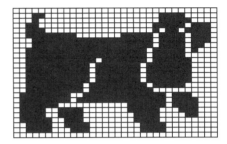

COCKER SPANIEL
30 x 24

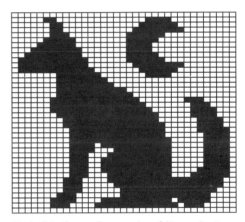

Knit this dog and moon in white against a midnight background.
33 x 38

34 x 5

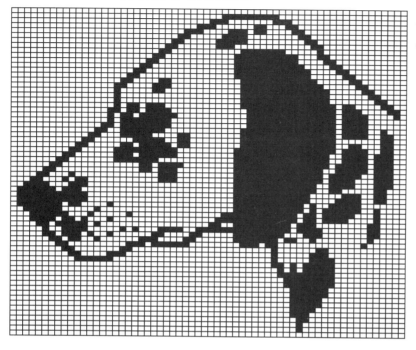

DALMATIAN
60 x 64

BASSET HOUND
60 x 86

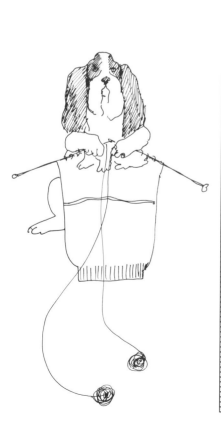

DALMATIAN
60 x 107

BORDER COLLIE
60 x 46

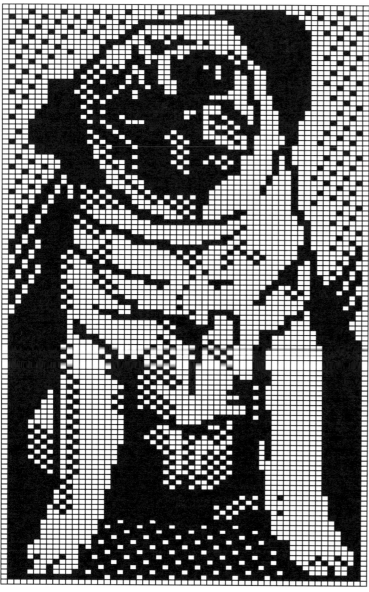

PUG
There's a pug on a red scarf on page 46.
55 x 114

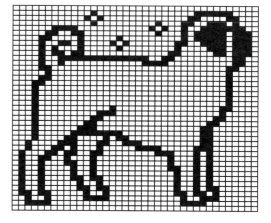

36 x 39

POODLE
This poodle is best suited for machine-knit Fair Isle.
60 x 92

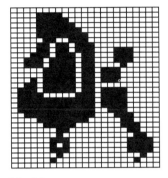

21 x 30

The little poodle is on a cap on page 48.

53 x 61

GERMAN SHEPHERD
60 x 83

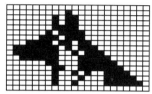

20 x 15

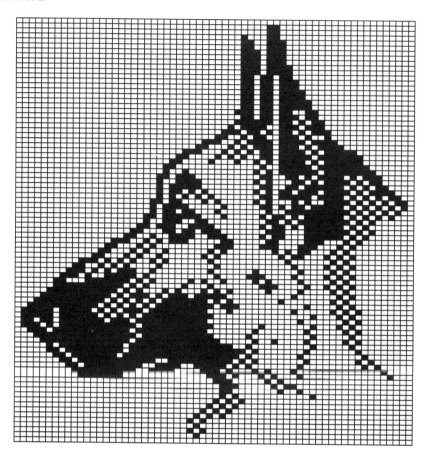

BULL TERRIER
56 x 57

LITTLE BULL TERRIERS
Knit the tongues pink.

16 x 32   16 x 32

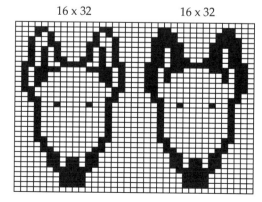

Horses

According to some people, horses are glorious and noble creatures, godlike in their grace and strength. According to others, they are stupid, but the people with this opinion may just be standing in the wrong corner of the paddock. The divine horse Epona was carved into the chalk undersoil at Uffington, England, in the pre-Christian era, and is admired by tourists today. Horse deities were common in European pagan religions, appearing as Pegasus, centaurs, death-goddesses, and fertility gods. The Roman cavalry adopted a horse-goddess as their protector. Here are some charts for hippophiles.

TROTTING ALONG
60 x 45

DRAFT HORSE
60 x 79

26 x 5

HORSESHOES

7 x 8   8 x 10   8 x 10

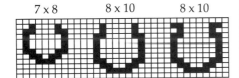

ARABIAN
61 x 139

JUMPER
50 x 57

DRESSAGE
58 x 65

CHESTNUT
59 x 126

MARE AND FOAL
These are shown on a sweater on page 43.
60 x 56

Livestock

Next time there is a state or county fair nearby, spend an afternoon cruising the livestock halls. Farm animals can have as much personality and sentience as the wisest family dog. When devoted owners give their great beasts the full cosmetic makeover (shampoos, mousse, nail polish, curling irons, five sorts of brushes and combs, perfume, powder, maybe a little hair dye for touch-up), they are startlingly beautiful. They would sit on your living room sofa, drink tea, and discuss Proust, if they could just fit through the doorway. Here are charts of some sociable beasts, large and small.

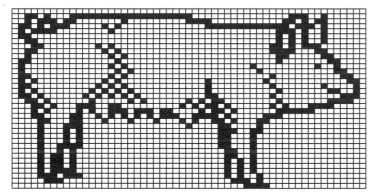

LANDRACE PIG
53 x 35

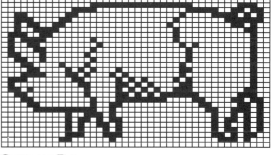

CHESHIRE PIG
40 x 28

PIG
24 x 19

15 x 5   17 x 5   16 x 5

MOO OINK BAA

MAMA HOLSTEIN
51 x 50

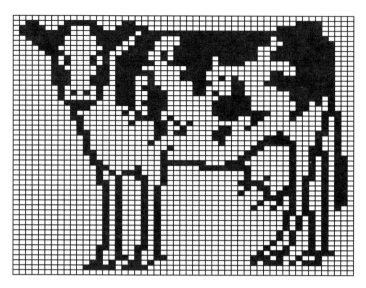

MAMA HEREFORD
60 x 49

NUBIAN GOAT
55 x 79

BULL
36 x 25

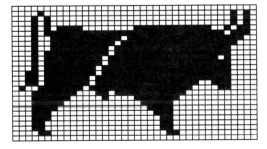

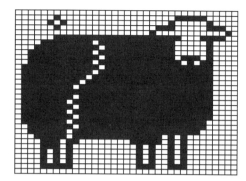

Scottish sheep come in many shades of gray, brown, and black.

SCOTTISH EWE
33 x 31

SCOTTISH RAM
33 x 39

SHEEP
16 x 14

BLACK LAMB
23 x 25

Knit this sheep in white with a dark ground.
24 x 26

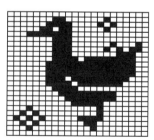

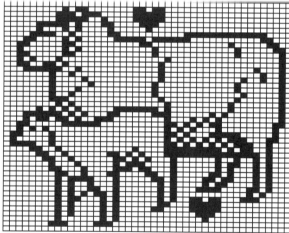

SHEEP AND LAMB
43 x 44

DUCK
20 x 19

Knit this duck white against a dark ground.
20 x 23

Rabbits

The Mimbres people, who lived in the pre-Columbian American Southwest, saw a rabbit in the moon; so did people in pre-Christian northern Europe. The moon-hare was the totem of the Saxon goddess of spring, Eostre. Eostre's name came from Ostara, a Teutonic goddess whose escort was a rabbit. These creatures are still with us in the rather less mystical form of the Easter bunny. Here are two rabbits ready to spring into sweaters.

Make this rabbit's eyes pink with a few duplicate stitches. Actually, this whole bunny can be worked in duplicate stitch.
59 x 75

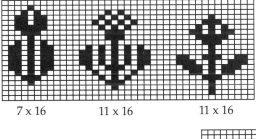

7 x 16   11 x 16   11 x 16

Here are flowers for the rabbit to run through . . . and a carrot . . .

5 x 5

7 x 18

The dots allow this rabbit to be a repeating pattern without long floats between the sets of ears. If you want just one rabbit, skip the dots. See this rabbit on a sweater on page 36.
60 x 58

Hometown

Combine these little charts to make a sweater that depicts a hometown. If you are machine knitting, use the charts in rows of color on white, or white on color, or lay them out as a landscape. If you are hand knitting, you have much more freedom in laying the town onto the sweater; knit in a row of several sorts of flowers, a road with two dif-

ferent cars, a row of different-colored houses. Have fun with these, and try charting your own whereabouts. There are distinctive buildings where you live, and buildings are easy to chart. If these buildings don't seem just right for your sweater, change them a little or a lot. After all, these are mostly from Cleveland.

SUNSET
31 x 15

UNIVERSITY
22 x 36

BIG HOUSE
23 x 28

TREE
11 x 17

POST OFFICE
19 x 28

RAILROAD
STATION
22 x 21

CHURCH
22 x 50

LIGHTHOUSE
20 x 37

TOWN HALL
17 x 36

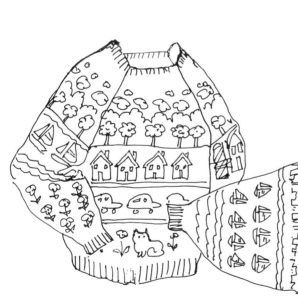

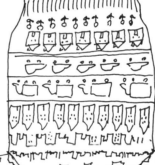

Put the horizon line at the bottom of the raglan yoke, so the sky will go up your shoulders.

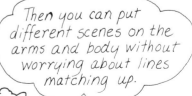

Then you can put different scenes on the arms and body without worrying about lines matching up.

Browse through the book, or check the index, to find other small patterns which can help make a very personal landscape: wild animals, farm animals, dogs and cats, boats, water, tennis rackets. . . . For an example, see the vest on page 43.

CLOUDS
34 x 20

LITTLE
HOUSES

12 x 18   13 x 17

FARM   16 x 25   12 x 25

CITY
59 x 18

CITY
HOUSES

11 x 20   9 x 20

GARDEN

9 x 12   9 x 12   9 x 12

TRUCKS

18 x 8   11 x 9

CARS

11 x 7   16 x 7

OH WOW IT'S GOT MY HOUSE AND MY SCHOOL AND MY KITTY!

Oak, Mistletoe, and Holly

The Oak God was central to the practices of the Druids, and mistletoe was ritually cut from his trees with a crescent-moon–shaped sickle. The practice of kissing under the mistletoe might be a genteel substitute for the drunken orgies that surrounded some ancient mistletoe rites.

Holly represents the feminine principle, and in heraldry represents truth. It was also paired with the masculine ivy in the solstice festivals of the cult of Dionysus. The leaders of the early Christian church tried, without success, to put a stop to the old pagan practice, which is celebrated in the songs "Deck the Hall" and "The Holly and the Ivy."

These oak, mistletoe, and holly charts are useful knitted down a sleeve or under a row of deer.

OAK
Knit the oak leaves green. Knit the acorns brown. The full repeat of the oak pattern is on the next page.
53 x 111

HOLLY
Sew big French knots in red to make holly berries at the ends of the stems.
83 x 20

The repeated oak pattern measures 105 stitches x 111 rows.

MISTLETOE
Sew big French knots in off-white to make mistletoe berries; look at a sprig of mistletoe—or page 42—to see where the berries should be.
95 x 55

Ships and Boats

People don't just sail or own boats; they fall in love with them. Knit a boat sweater for someone you know who is suffering from an attack of boat lust. Remember that wool can absorb a great deal of moisture and not feel wet; by contrast, damp cotton feels clammy, and rubs and sags.

DISTANT MOUNTAINS
50 x 11

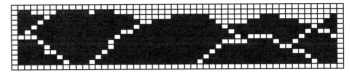

CLOSE HILLS
53 x 9

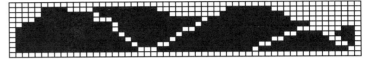

CLOUDS
25 x 20

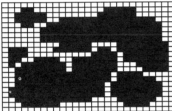

WAVES BREAKING ON A BEACH
10 x 14

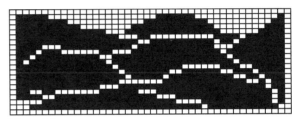

NEAR MOUNTAINS
42 x 19

60 x 82

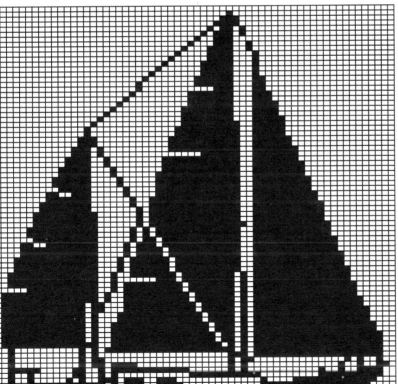

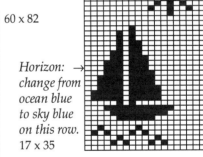

Horizon: → change from ocean blue to sky blue on this row.
17 x 35

BEACH DUNES
9 x 4   11 x 3

SHALLOW WATER
27 x 6

DEEP WATER
34 x 10

133

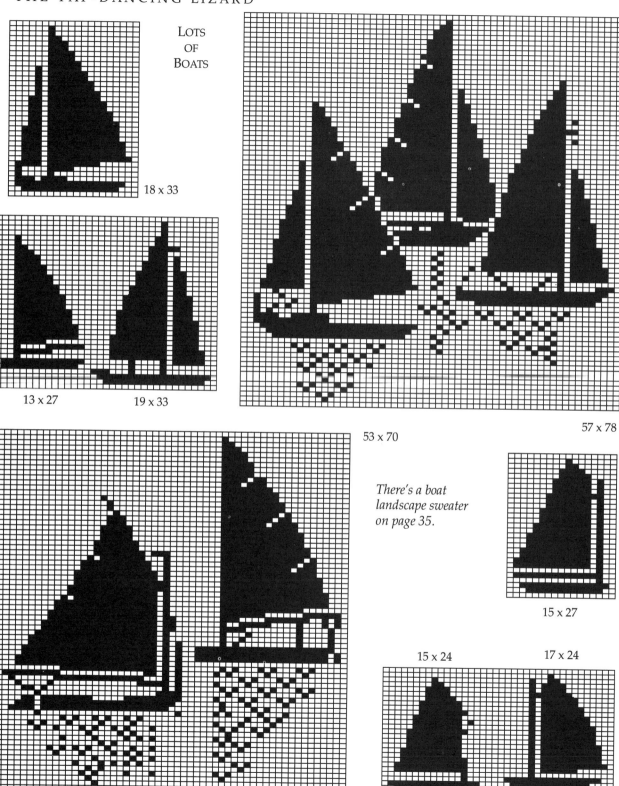

LOTS
OF
BOATS

18 x 33

13 x 27   19 x 33

53 x 70

57 x 78

*There's a boat
landscape sweater
on page 35.*

15 x 27

15 x 24   17 x 24

Trees

People have always loved trees. They shade us, clean the air, give us fuel, shelter, and food, and are comforting to lean against. We used these charts to knit a four-seasons tree cape. The spring quarter was embroidered with dusty pink French knots to suggest a crab apple tree in bloom. The summer quarter was knitted as a leafy tree. The autumn quarter was embroidered in larger French knots to represent a tree loaded with crab apples. The winter quarter was knitted as a bare-branched tree.

These are the trees as full repeats; their half patterns are on the next two pages. Each tree measures 120 stitches by 150 rows.

The trunk of the tree above is just a line; it's eight stitches wide at the bottom, and tapers up as long as your knitting will allow.

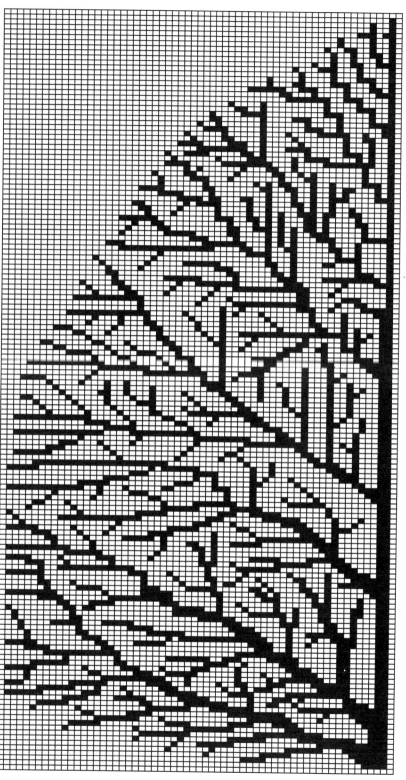

These drafts could represent a couple of different species of trees: with buds in the spring, green leaves in the summer, golden leaves in the autumn, and bare limbs in the winter.

60 x 150

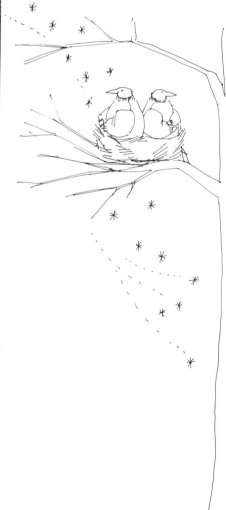

Try making a lovely crabapple tree, with pink French knots all over the branches for a spring tree, dark green knots as foliage for summer, red knots in the autumn, and bare branches in deep winter.

60 x 150

The heavens

Moon

Humans have always had mixed feelings about the moon. Some primitive peoples believed it was more important than the sun. After all, the moon shines during the night, when light is useful, whereas the sun wastes its time shining when the sky is already lit. Medieval Europeans distrusted the moon. An anonymous German poet of the time wrote that fortune was "like the moon, always changing," providing composer Carl Orff with the text for the first section of his cantata, *Carmina Burana.* Every sailor knew that the tides changed according to the phase of the moon, and since water was a "feminine element" according to ancient science and occult practice, it was assumed that women were as much under the spell of the moon as the seas were. Some women do indeed "howl at the moon." In some cultures, that is their joy and strength; in others, it is their weakness. Moonlight was considered dangerous, a source of madness, and even as late as the "Age of Enlightenment," physicians were warning their patients not to let the light of the moon fall on their beds as they slept.

This moon chart has rays and stars to keep floats to a minimum in Fair Isle work. Knit it in white on black. Consider sparkling it up with silvered rocaille and tube beads sewn over the stars and lines.

60 x 150

Stars

The ubiquitous knitted "snowflakes" are in reality folk patterns representing stars. There are so many beautiful stars in folk embroidery that it is difficult to chart anything new, but because they are so useful in knitting, some are included here along with their ancestry.

The first star of this shape was a symbol for the goddess Ishtar, Babylonian goddess of love and war. Since Ishtar was a popular goddess with mystic connections to Aphrodite, Astarte, and Esther, and the star was very easy to "count" in weaving and embroidery, it appeared in many textiles. The stars traveled wherever Middle Eastern textiles were traded, and because they were beautiful and adaptable, weavers, embroiderers, and knitters copied them into local textiles far from their source. Where Ishtar was unknown or forgotten, the stars were given other names reflecting the needs and culture into which they had been adapted. Christians called particularly large and intricate stars the "Star of Bethlehem." In Nordic countries, they were called "snowflakes."

SINGLE STARS.
These can be repeated with spaces in between.

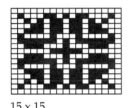

15 x 15

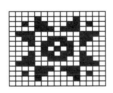

13 x 13

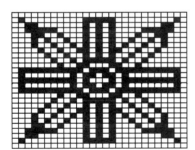

25 x 25

22 x 22

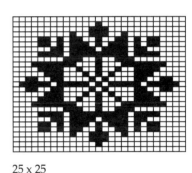

25 x 25

BANDS OF STARS.
These are designed to be used in repeats.

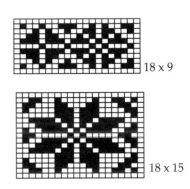

18 x 9

18 x 15

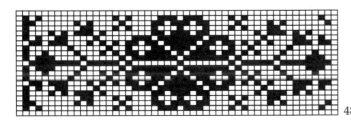

48 x 19

Sun

There are billions of stars in the known universe but only one sun. Astronomers tell us it is just another star and not a particularly remarkable one, but we still believe it is special—after all, out of the billions of stars, this one is ours.

Most early sun symbols are circular, with either a dot in the middle or concentric rays projecting from the center. The rays are often bent or curved. This is the source of the triskelion, a symbol with three curved branches (common in Aegean and Celtic decorative art), and the four-branched swastika (from the Sanskrit "so be it"), which before becoming the symbol of German Nazism in the 1920s and 1930s was a solar symbol found worldwide since at least 10,000 B.C.

The sun has been regarded both as male and as female, depending on the culture of the era. In the West, both genders have had a fling at being the solar deity or spirit, but in the popular imagination of today, the male figures (such as Apollo and Horus) are most familiar. In many schools of occult study, the sun's most apparent characteristics—warmth, dryness, energy, stability, and brilliance—have been considered masculine attributes, and these notions continue to shape our thinking. Sun faces in art tend to be masculine; artists merge beards and flames, make the sun look wise, patient, enlightened, and kingly; more than one artist has made the sun look decidedly like a self-portrait.

The large sun chart here knits well in Fair Isle technique, in fiery colors. This might be a good chart on which to try out the skeins of metallic yarn you've been saving. If you're knitting this by hand or on a machine in intarsia technique, consider filling areas of the face and flames in different fiery colors. To visualize this, make photocopies of the sunface and color them with crayons until you have one you want to knit. Sew gold rocaille beads along the lines in the face to make it shimmer.

The full sun pattern measures 118 stitches by 123 rows. The half pattern is on the next page, and a sweater is on page 34.

59 x 123

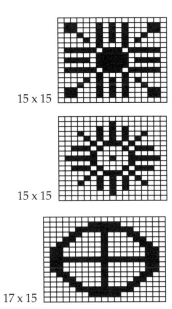

15 x 15

15 x 15

17 x 15

Soar Away

There are few musical experiences that can match listening to, or better yet singing with, a group of shape-note singers. Shape-note, or "Sacred Harp," music began as a form of popular education and entertainment in the Northeast in early America. The notes were written using different shapes to represent pitches. The tradition of shape-note singing continues today in the South, although groups of shape-note singers gather throughout the United States. The annual "Big Singing" at Benton, Kentucky, is one of the most important shape-note conventions.

This sweater was inspired by a shape-note tune called "Soar Away," written in the 1920s by A. Marcus Cagle.

If your knitting machine knits at nine to ten rows per inch, you can knit these wings.

The designs on your garments should reflect your interests. This sweater was inspired by a song from the shape-note tradition of four-part vocal harmony. The lyrics of the chorus go: "I'd soar away above the sky, I'd fly and fly, to see my God above." Think about the things that mean a lot to you, and how they might be incorporated into a piece of clothing.

This chart looks especially good knitted as a white-winged heart on a dark background.

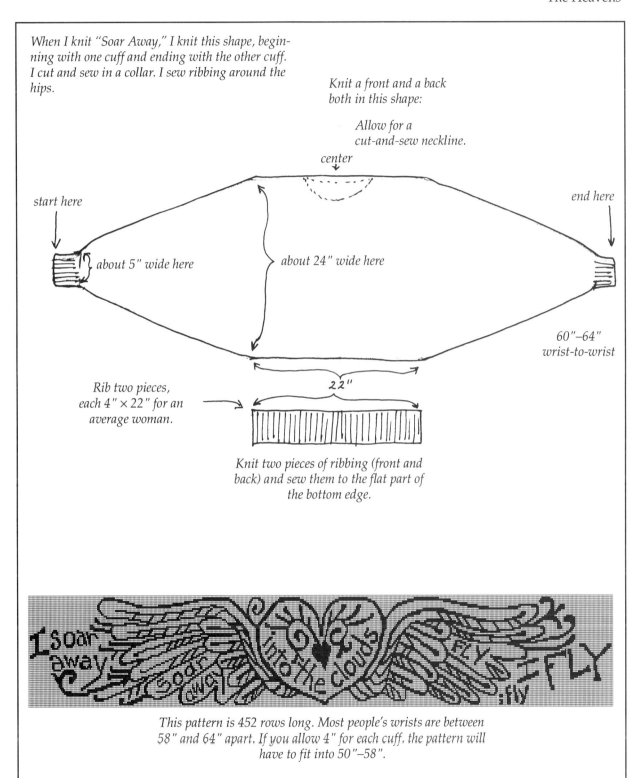

When I knit "Soar Away," I knit this shape, beginning with one cuff and ending with the other cuff. I cut and sew in a collar. I sew ribbing around the hips.

Knit a front and a back both in this shape:

Allow for a cut-and-sew neckline.

center

start here

about 5" wide here

about 24" wide here

end here

60"–64" wrist-to-wrist

Rib two pieces, each 4" × 22" for an average woman.

22"

Knit two pieces of ribbing (front and back) and sew them to the flat part of the bottom edge.

This pattern is 452 rows long. Most people's wrists are between 58" and 64" apart. If you allow 4" for each cuff, the pattern will have to fit into 50"–58".

60 x 152

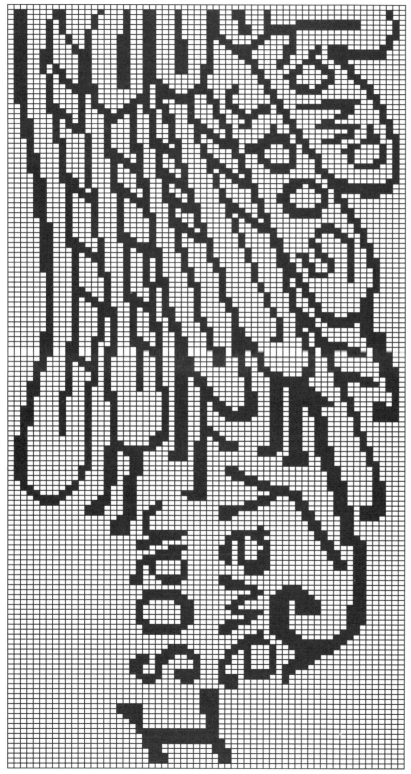

60 x 150

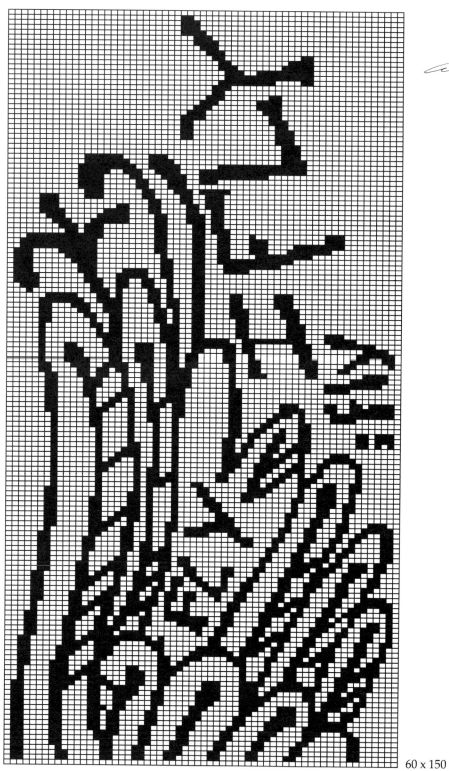

60 x 150

At home

Flowers

Every spring and summer, some days are chilly enough to make you run for a sweater. The sweaters in the drawer, however, all look so *wintry!* Here are charts of lovely spring flowers to knit into something you can wear when the calendar says "blissful warmth" but the weatherman says, "Cover your tomatoes."

60 x 120

TULIP.
See the doubled pattern opposite.

← *Change color this row.*

LILY OF THE VALLEY.
Hand-embroider the white flowers in place, as you can see on the sleeves of the sweater on page 34.

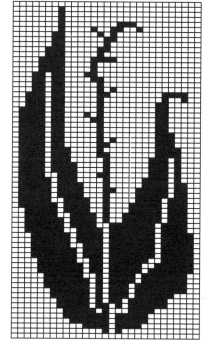

27 x 65

TULIP

DAYLILY

The doubled daylily pattern measures 119 stitches x 150 rows. See the half pattern on the next page.

Sew big French knots in gold to look like stamens in the lily blossom; see the sweater on page 34 for ideas about embroidered details.

DAYLILY.
60 x 150

← *Change color this row.*

Little flowers

11 x 21

13 x 22

WATER LILY.
Knit the lily with a white blossom and jade leaves against deep blue water. Note that the water ripples are a stitch wider than the lily; both patterns should have the same center line, but the width of your knitting will be calculated to fit the ripple area.
59 x 144

The doubled pattern is on the next page, and a dress is on page 35.

← *Change color this row.*

WATER RIPPLES BELOW LILY.
60 x 12

The doubled water lily and ripple patterns need 119 stitches of fabric width; there can be a varying number of rows between the two elements, but if you use 3 blank rows, the full depth of the design will be 159 rows (144 for lily, 3 for transition, and 12 for ripples).

More little flowers.

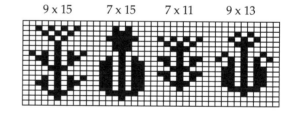

9 x 15   7 x 15   7 x 11   9 x 13

13 x 18   9 x 15   9 x 15   9 x 15   9 x 15

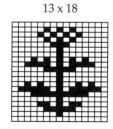

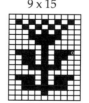

Christmas

Here are patterns for Christmas sweaters and Christmas stockings. One of the lesser Germanic goddesses was Berchta, an old woman whose domain was the hearth. Mothers, trying to get their daughters to tend to their spinning and knitting lessons, would threaten that Berchta was watching them secretly at night. Berchta was fond of small children, but punished those who were not industrious . . . does this sound familiar? Berchta was around a long time ago, before Christianity came to Europe.

Christmas patterns and stars (page 141) make classic Christmas stockings.

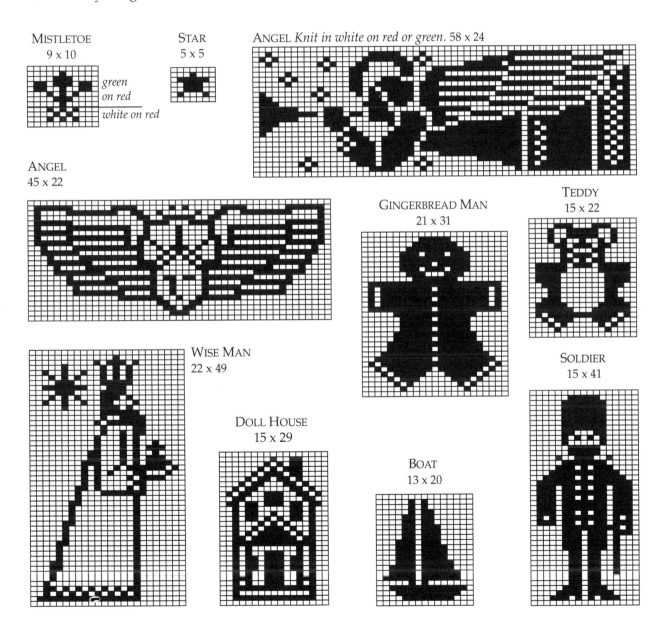

MISTLETOE
9 x 10

green on red

white on red

STAR
5 x 5

ANGEL *Knit in white on red or green.* 58 x 24

ANGEL
45 x 22

GINGERBREAD MAN
21 x 31

TEDDY
15 x 22

WISE MAN
22 x 49

DOLL HOUSE
15 x 29

BOAT
13 x 20

SOLDIER
15 x 41

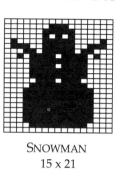

SNOWMAN
15 x 21

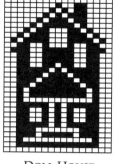

DOLL HOUSE
15 x 29

TEDDY
17 x 26

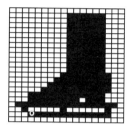

ICE SKATE
16 x 21

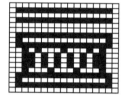

DRUM
15 x 16

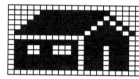

CABIN
19 x 12

ROCKING HORSE
20 x 20

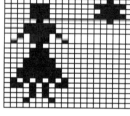

DOLLY   STAR
9 x 20   5 x 5

*green
on red*
_____
white on red

MISTLETOE
11 x 10

DEER
19 x 26

TREE
11 x 18

SNOWMAN
20 x 33
*Sew and knot yarn
around snowmen's necks
to make scarves.*

JULIE'S TRAIN
40 x 30

TREE
15 x 31

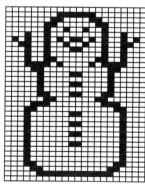

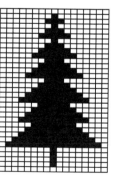

156

A fast flatbed Christmas stocking

1. Make the fabric.

End at 25"–30", with an unfinished edge

2. Press the knitted stocking flat with plenty of steam and ironing. Then sew the heel into shape.

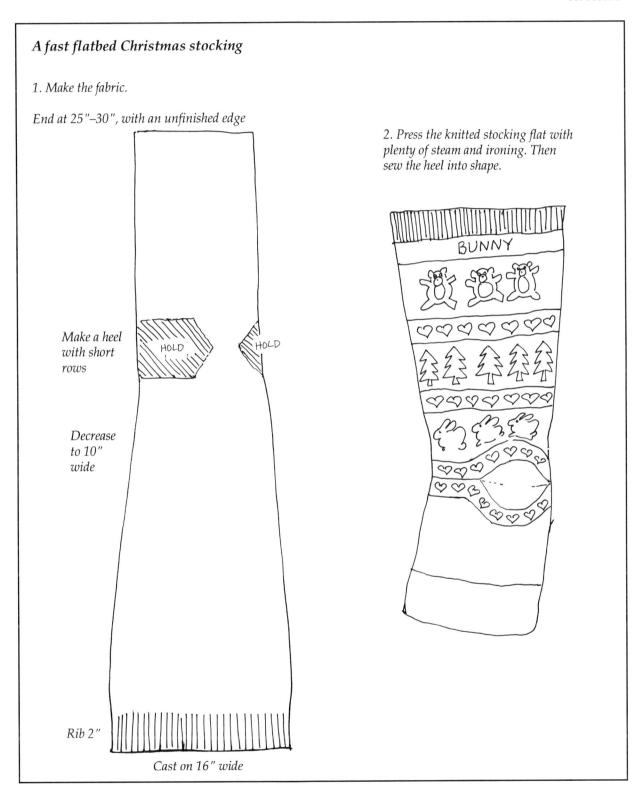

Make a heel with short rows

HOLD   HOLD

BUNNY

Decrease to 10" wide

Rib 2"

Cast on 16" wide

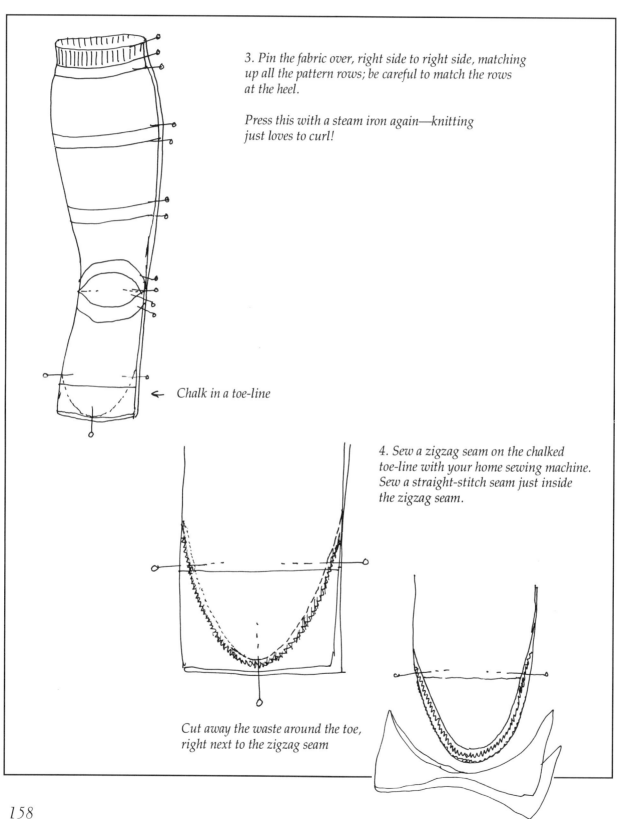

3. Pin the fabric over, right side to right side, matching up all the pattern rows; be careful to match the rows at the heel.

Press this with a steam iron again—knitting just loves to curl!

← *Chalk in a toe-line*

4. Sew a zigzag seam on the chalked toe-line with your home sewing machine. Sew a straight-stitch seam just inside the zigzag seam.

Cut away the waste around the toe, right next to the zigzag seam

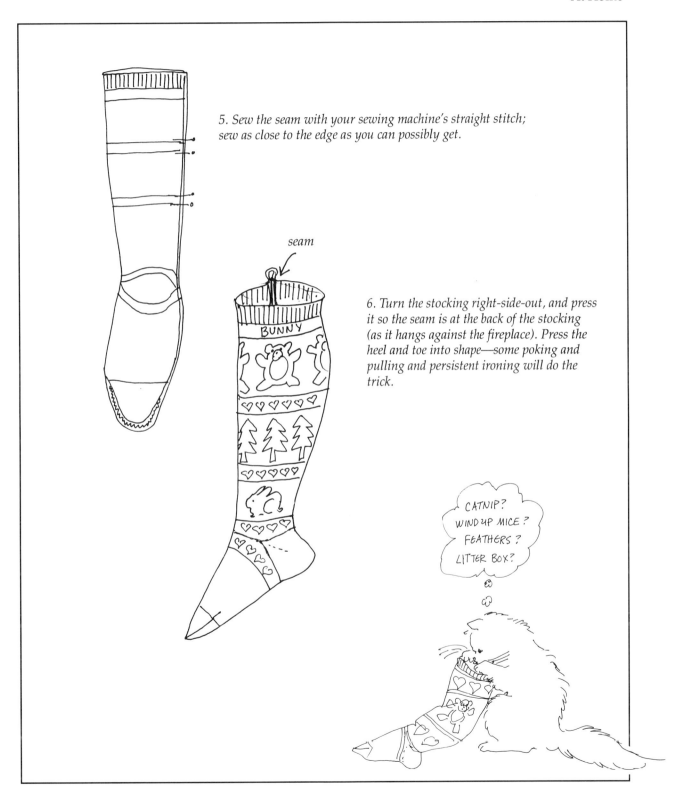

5. *Sew the seam with your sewing machine's straight stitch; sew as close to the edge as you can possibly get.*

seam

6. *Turn the stocking right-side-out, and press it so the seam is at the back of the stocking (as it hangs against the fireplace). Press the heel and toe into shape—some poking and pulling and persistent ironing will do the trick.*

BUNNY

CATNIP?
WIND UP MICE?
FEATHERS?
LITTER BOX?

Little Patterns and Miscellaneous Treats

Everyone who wants a sweater custom knitted wants a little something special. Here is a collection of "something specials." Some are especially useful when knitting a "Gramma" sweater—a sweater which has all the grandchildren's names, each with a row of something that grandchild likes. One of these might be what you need to knit the curious thing you dearly love into a treasured sweater.

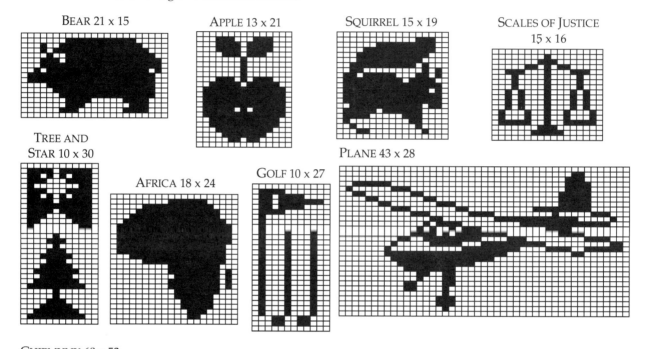

BEAR 21 x 15

APPLE 13 x 21

SQUIRREL 15 x 19

SCALES OF JUSTICE 15 x 16

TREE AND STAR 10 x 30

AFRICA 18 x 24

GOLF 10 x 27

PLANE 43 x 28

CHIPMUNK 60 x 53

PALM TREE AND STARS 17 x 45

FOOTBALL 25 x 15

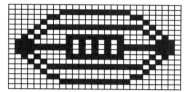

SOCCER BALL
15 x 15

HEDGEHOG
60 x 39

LIFE-
PRESERVER
17 x 15

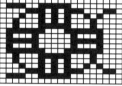

TENNIS
21 x 30

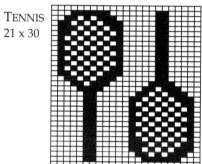

FRENCH HORN 60 x 85

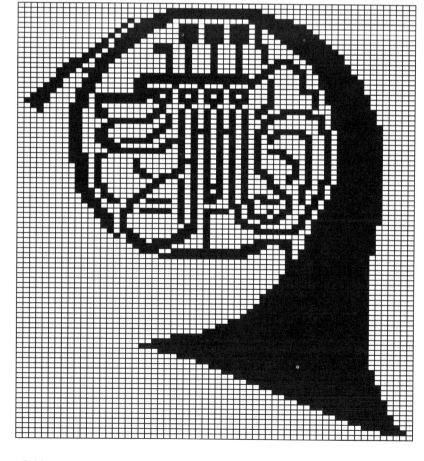

ANCHOR
11 x 16

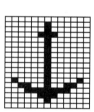

BALLET
SLIPPER
10 x 38

VIOLIN,
CELLO, OR
BASS (IT'S ALL
RELATIVE!)
11 x 31

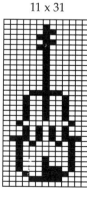

Elaborations

Computers

This may be the "computer age," and high-tech machines may be all around us, but many people, particularly artistic and creative people, suffer anxiety attacks when confronted with a computer they have to operate themselves. The mere mention of computers can scare an artistic soul (note that we put this section near the back of the book).

However, knitting, even for the dabbler, has been changed by the growth of computer technology. Whether you are a hand or machine knitter, you can use computers to draft patterns and maintain files of patterns in a neater and more convenient form than a tumbledown stack of knitting magazines sitting in a closet. Knitting machines with small, built-in pattern computers have been available for years, and more sophisticated machines which can be connected directly to a personal computer are now within the means of many home-based professionals and even casual knitters.

If you are a machine knitter and you have been thinking about investing in one of these new, flashy, computer-controlled models, close your purse, take ten deep breaths, look at your present machine, and ask yourself, "Would the new machine extend my technique and let me knit things I want to knit but can't knit now?" If the answer is "No," then go apologize to your trusty old punchcard knitter for even thinking of trading it in, and take heart: a lot of excellent knitting is still being done with the old machines, while many of the people using the new ones have never managed to get beyond twenty-four–stitch repeats. However, if you have ideas that are beyond the powers of your present machine (for example, we are experimenting with asymmetrical, nonrepeating, single-unit patterns knitted sideways), or if you are a hand knitter interested in trying space-age technology on for size, it might be time to trade up.

If you are an experienced machine knitter, the choice of a machine will be relatively easy, because you already have some idea of what is available, you know what you want the machine to do, and you have probably developed a loyalty to whatever brand you are using. If you are a beginner, the choice is still not too difficult, because there are only a few knitting machine manufacturers and not all of them have brought out computer knitters.

Things get more complicated after you have decided on a machine, because you also must choose the accessories ("peripherals") which will let you tap the machine's brainpower. Depending on the make and model of your machine, these may include pattern design computers, video monitors, disk drives, and printers. If confusion is setting in, a few definitions may be in order.

Pattern design computer: This is a small keyboard unit which connects to your knitting machine and "talks" to its inboard computer. It is a useful tool for designing your own patterns or modifying the manufacturer's built-in patterns.

Video monitor: This may be as simple as a color TV. Using only the pattern computer, you are working blind and have no easy way of spotting errors in your pattern until you knit it. A monitor hooked up to the knitting machine and pattern computer will allow you to see the pattern in color as you design it and to view your progress as you knit.

Disk drive: This is a device which stores data on small disks of magnetic material. The knitting machine has a built-in memory, but it is limited and volatile: that is, it goes blank as soon as the power is shut off. Some machines have a long-life battery installed to help preserve their memory while they're shut off, but batteries run down eventually. A knitting machine disk drive using 3.5-inch "micro disks" can hold more than a half-million stitches on one disk, and any pattern can be stored on the disk or recalled with a few keystrokes on the knitting machine's computer.

Printer: Another way to preserve a design is to make a hard copy (printed on paper). A computer printer connected to the knitting machine lets you print out your patterns. This can be useful for big projects or for sharing ideas with other knitters.

A computer knitting machine fully equipped with all these accessories is enough to keep even the most imaginative knitter busy, but there will always be those who want more. For these folks, companies which specialize in computer knitting paraphernalia offer software packages for designing knits on a personal computer and an interface to send the finished designs to the inboard computer in your knitting machine. This setup is typically faster and more flexible than the proprietary hardware and software packages your knitting machine dealer has for sale, but it is much more expensive, unless you already have a computer. If you do, your only additional expense beyond the knitting machine will be the software and interface.

Another thing to consider is the time and effort you have to devote to learning how to operate a fairly complex system. The skills are well within the range of anyone who can read a complex knitting chart, but mastering the system means learning a new language and new techniques. The payoff for the extra expense and trouble is a computer-aided design (CAD) system that you can use to plan and execute patterns you could only have dreamed of a few years ago.

If you are a hand knitter, you need not feel that this new technology has nothing to offer you. Although the focus in computer knitting software design has been on the knitting machine, computers can be used to chart and store patterns for hand knitters, who incidentally have an advantage over those of us who use machines: a pair of needles is a lot cheaper. If you own or have access to a computer, a number of art or "paint" programs allow you to set up a grid on your screen which approximates your knitting gauge. Then you can design your sweater on the grid in colors to match your yarns. If you have a color printer, you can print the designs as they appear on the screen; with a black-and-white printer, you can arrange to have the printer use grays and crosshatches to represent the colors.

You have probably noticed that, in spite of the expense of a CAD system, we have not mentioned specific prices. Computer prices fluctuate greatly. What seems to be a good deal today could look like less of a bargain a few months from now. Changes in international exchange rates and in the supplies of imported circuit components can cause sudden changes in price. Fierce competition among manufacturers is another problem for anyone trying to predict the price of equipment, although it has been a boon to small-time computer users. New technology is driving older, though quite serviceable, technology off the market at an alarming rate. Those of us who are happy to make do with the "obsolete" equipment have done quite well buying our hardware at rock-bottom prices on the closeout market. This requires some careful shopping, however; you need to be sure that the equipment you buy will still receive technical support from the manufacturer and will run whatever software you need to use. If you are a computer novice, it is best to go shopping with an experienced friend.

Though it can do some pretty spectacular things, the computer is only a tool; it is no substitute for creativity, imagination, and hard work. The same rule applies to buying computer knitting equipment as to buying other tools: get a good idea of what you want the tool to do for you, shop carefully with that purpose in mind, and buy the best-quality tools you can afford to meet your needs.

Selected Bibliography

Whether you are a hand or a machine knitter, if you want your knitting to make people take notice and wonder where you managed to find such beautiful and unusual patterns, you need to look beyond knitting books and bring the larger world of images and symbols within reach of your needles. The patterns in this book represent years of reading, trips to museum exhibitions, leafing through picture books, and sketching anything that looked interesting.

Books are an especially good source of ideas for those of us not wealthy enough to roam the world looking for the perfect sweater pattern. In these days of easy photocopying, a lifetime's worth of design ideas can be gleaned from a few visits to a public library, and there is at least one publisher which prints a special series of designs with few copyright restrictions with artists and craftspeople in mind (more on that later). It also helps to read about history, culture, religion, myth, and magic. Learn what you can about the customs of other peoples. This background reading will prepare your mind for what you will discover when you search for new ideas.

To get started, here is a list, sorted by topics, of the books which provided information and inspired patterns for this book, and of some books we turn to when we need to set the mental gears in motion.

The Craft

Knitting and needlework

The first four books in this list include most of the information you probably wish had been printed in the manual that came with your knitting machine.

Cartwright-Jones, Catherine. *The Prolific Knitting Machine.* Loveland, Colorado: Interweave Press, 1990.

We include this title not as a plug, but as a suggestion to readers who want to see the sweater shapes we have been using to carry the patterns shown in this book.

Kinder, Kathleen. *Techniques in Machine Knitting.* London: B. T. Batsford, 1985.

This book discusses a wide range of techniques and applications for both single- and double-bed machines. The chapter on lace making is one of the best in the literature.

Lewis, Susanna, and Julia Weissman. *A Machine Knitter's Guide to Creating Fabrics.* New York: Sterling, 1986.

This book concentrates on fabric design, rather than knitting technique or garment design. It provides general information on a lot of sample fabrics, as well as specifics for making them on different machine models.

Nabney, Janet. *An Illustrated Handbook of Machine Knitting.* London: B. T. Batsford, 1987.

This is a good book for machine knitters who ask themselves how (or why) their machines work as they do. It explains not only how to do many basic and fancy stitches, but also gives illustrations to show how the machine goes about its work.

Norbury, James. *Traditional Knitting Patterns from Scandinavia, the British Isles, France, Italy, and Other European Countries.* New York: Dover, 1973.

Norbury gives charts and instructions for over two hundred knitting patterns.

Rutt, Richard. *A History of Handknitting.* Loveland, Colorado: Interweave Press, 1988.

Anglican bishop and knitting enthusiast Richard Rutt covers a surprising amount of information (including history, charts, techniques, traditions, and noted knitting personalities) in a single, readable volume.

Thomas, Mary. *Mary Thomas's Knitting Book.* New York: Dover, 1972.

This republication of a 1938 manual by one of Britain's best-known handknitting experts includes basic stitch techniques and garment designs, and can help beginners get started as well as serve as a valuable reference work for experienced knitters.

Thomas, Mary. *Mary Thomas's Book of Knitting Patterns*. New York: Dover, 1972.

This book covers nearly everything that can be done with a pair of needles, from simple knit and purl stitches to complex laces and ornamental techniques.

Clothing design

Bullen, Nicholas. *Making Lingerie and Nightwear*. London: Mills and Boon, 1979.

If you have tried lace making on your knitting machine and you are looking for an interesting project, buy some light cotton or silk (around five thousand yards per pound) and try your hand at one of these designs. Knitted in a heavier yarn in Fair Isle technique, some of the patterns also make interesting outerwear. Bullen's patterns are intended for home sewing, but many adapt well to knitting, and make it easy to produce rich-looking garments with a minimum of time and money.

Burnham, Dorothy K. *Cut My Cote*. Toronto: The Royal Ontario Museum, 1973.

This is a brief description of the evolution of traditional coat and shirt design, including diagrams of the methods used to lay out and cut a number of garments included in the Royal Ontario Museum textile collection.

Michelson, Carmen, and Mary-Ann Davis. *The Knitter's Guide to Sweater Design*. Loveland, Colorado: Interweave Press, 1989.

If you want to experiment with different shapes in knitting, check out this book. Michelson and Davis show how to knit many simple and complex body, sleeve, and collar types, and how to calculate sizes and yardage.

Tilke, Max. *Costume Patterns and Designs*. New York: Rizzoli International, 1990.

Tilke died before completing this companion volume to A Pictorial History of Costume, *which he co-wrote with Wolfgang Bruhn, but the results are nonetheless magnificent. Tilke's color plates show the shapes and decorative details of traditional and historical costumes from Europe, Asia, North Africa, and the Americas.*

Visual Culture, by Regions

Africa

Picton, John. *African Textiles*. New York: Harper Collins, 1989.

Many motifs used by African weavers can be adapted to knitting by anyone willing to take the time to chart the patterns. This book contains dozens of color and black-and-white photographs which should inspire any knitter looking for something out of the ordinary.

Revault, Jacques. *Designs and Patterns from North African Carpets and Textiles*. New York: Dover, 1973.

Revault catalogued hundreds of designs, most of them from Tunisia; over three hundred patterns are included in this book, and many are charted. The text includes the names and significance of many of the motifs.

Rossini, Stephane. *Egyptian Hieroglyphics: How to Read and Write Them*. New York: Dover, 1989.

Part of the fascination of the early written Egyptian language is that it is so beautiful to look at. Rossini provides large, clear pictures of the individual hieroglyphics, as well as pronunciation keys and sample words. Try personalizing your next sweater in the language of the pharaohs.

Williams, Geoffrey. *African Designs from Traditional Sources*. New York: Dover, 1971.

There are nearly four hundred designs in this collection of patterns gathered from sub-Saharan African peoples, ranging from printed fabric motifs to complex sculptures. All are rendered in black-and-white block print form, making them easy to adapt to almost any design project.

Wilson, Eva. *Ancient Egyptian Designs for Artists and Craftspeople*. New York: Dover, 1987.

This is a collection of over four hundred black-and-white illustrations showing details of pottery, jewelry, basketry, and other Egyptian artifacts. The book includes a history of Egyptian decorative arts and a brief description of each example.

The Americas

Appleton, Leroy H. *American Indian Design and Decoration*. New York: Dover, 1971.

Appleton brings together the history, myths, legends, and poetry of the native peoples of the Americas as the background for over seven hundred design motifs collected from all over the Western Hemisphere.

Jessen, Ellen. *Peruvian Designs for Cross-Stitch*. New York: Van Nostrand Reinhold, 1980.

The grids in this book are small and a little faint, but with perseverance and a magnifying glass you will be rewarded with wonderful abstract borders and animal figures charted from the finest of Native American decorated textiles.

Mera, H. P. *Pueblo Designs: One Hundred Seventy-Six Illustrations of the Rain Bird*. New York: Dover, 1970.

The "rain bird" is a common figure in Southwestern Indian pottery. Mera traces its history and gives scores of examples of how it appeared in different cultures. The loops, curves, and whorls of the rain bird designs are difficult to chart for knitting, but we have done a few, and the results have been worth the trouble.

Wasserman, Tamara E., and Jonathan S. Hill. *Bolivian Indian Textiles: Traditional Designs and Costumes*. New York: Dover, 1981.

The belts, pouches, and other weavings of the Bolivian people are a rich source of design ideas, especially for borders, stripes, and bands.

Asia and the Middle East

Amir, Ziva. *Arabesque: Decorative Needlework from the Holy Land.* Israel: Massada Press, 1977.

Middle Eastern Arab women embroider their garments with a great variety of representational and abstract patterns. Amir shows many of these patterns in context, explains how they are used, and presents them in chart form.

Hawley, W. M., ed. *Chinese Folk Designs: A Collection of 300 Cut-Paper Designs.* New York: Dover, 1971.

This is a collection of hua yang, *the embroidery designs used to decorate everyday objects. Hawley's collection shows them as the cut-paper patterns used to lay out the embroidery. Try enlarging or reducing an interesting pattern on a copier, then tracing it on a knitting grid.*

Kerimov, Lyatif. *Folk Designs from the Caucasus for Knitting and Needlework.* New York: Dover, 1974.

If you have any "oriental" carpets in your home, you might recognize some of these patterns. Kerimov catalogued the carpet patterns used by Azerbaijani weavers and published them in chart form. Machine knitters can bring these patterns to life with duplicate stitching. Hand knitters who can manage their bobbins well and choose good colors can produce some exciting results.

Tana, Pradumna, and Rosalba Tana. *Floral and Animal Stencil Designs from India.* New York: Dover, 1986.

With patience, these floral blends, birds, and animals reproduced from Indian temple art can be made into unusual knitting patterns, or can serve as inspiration for ideas of your own.

Europe

Needlework charts are a good source of patterns for knitters. We have used needlework collections for most of the traditional European patterns we have adapted to knitting. Here is a list of our favorite sources.

Bain, George. *Celtic Art: The Methods of Construction.* New York: Dover, 1973.

If Celtic art fascinates you and you would like to create designs of your own, this book is all you need to get started. Bain gives clear instructions for drawing the traditional forms of Celtic art, including step, key, knot, and fret patterns, as well as human and animal figures and calligraphic forms.

Geirl, Irmgard. *Cross Stitch Patterns.* London: B. T. Batsford, 1987.

Geirl concentrates on Swiss and Austrian patterns, drafted in a format that is remarkably easy to read.

Kiewe, Heinz Edgar. *Charted Peasant Designs from Saxon Transylvania.* New York: Dover, 1977.

This collection of patterns spans the history of needlework in central Europe from the eleventh century to the Art Nouveau period. It features good selections of continuous geometric bands and abstract animal forms.

Neubecker, Ottfried. *Heraldry: Sources, Symbols and Meaning.* New York: McGraw-Hill, 1976.

Occasionally we are asked to knit a family's arms into a sweater. This book has been a great help in getting all the details right. Every page is illustrated, mostly with details from historical pieces.

Sibmacher, Johan. *Baroque Charted Designs for Needlework.* New York: Dover, 1975.

This is a reproduction of a chartbook engraved and published in Nuremburg, Germany, in 1604. Hand and machine knitters will find useful ideas for attractive pattern bands in these ninety-nine illustrations, including mythical beasts, florals, and geometrics.

Spinhoven, Co. *Celtic Charted Designs.* New York: Dover, 1987.

The intricate knot and fretwork patterns of Celtic decorative art make intriguing sweater designs. Spinhoven's collection contains nearly four hundred designs from authentic sources in charted form.

Ideas and Perspectives

Even the most dedicated knitter sometimes has to get up from the machine or put down the needles. For these moments, here are two lists of books which offer ideas about the visible, invisible, and imaginary worlds and how they come together to produce traditional and mythical images.

Art and vision

Farris, Edmond J. *Art Students' Anatomy*. New York: Dover, 1961.

If more people who design and make clothing took a careful look at the shape, proportion, and structure of the human body, we would all have an easier time finding comfortable clothes to wear.

Franck, Fredrick. *The Zen of Seeing*. New York: Random House, 1973.

Franck's gentle, contemplative text and sketches will make you want to slow down and look more carefully at everything.

Itten, Johannes. *Itten: The Elements of Color*. New York: Van Nostrand Reinhold, 1970.

This small volume is drawn from the writings of Johannes Itten, one of the great color theorists of the twentieth century. It makes a good primer for anyone who wants to understand how and why colors work together.

Nicolaides, Kimon. *The Natural Way to Draw: A Working Plan for Art Study*. Boston: Houghton Mifflin, 1969.

If you want to design, you need to be able to draw. Nicolaides believed that learning to draw was chiefly a matter of learning how to look at the world. Nicolaides' book is a course in observation, with illustrations and exercises, which can teach anyone how to get an observation down on paper.

Samuels, Mike, and Nancy Samuels. *Seeing with the Mind's Eye: The History, Techniques and Uses of Visualization*. New York: Random House, 1975.

The traditional images we have adopted for our work and presented in this book, as well as those in the books in this bibliography, were, in many cases, the result of some person's visualization, either in a dream or a heightened waking state. Visualization has also been the source of many of the most important works in all of the arts. Mike and Nancy Samuels explain with words, pictures, and symbols how this curious mental faculty works and how we can use it.

Culture, myth, and magic

The symbols and images used to decorate clothing are usually more than pretty patterns. They have meanings that are often rooted in a culture's oldest traditions. While you are looking at traditional patterns, spend some time reading the old stories and myths and looking for the connections between what you read and what you see. You will begin to develop a sense of the grammar of symbols and ornaments, and then you will be on your way toward knitting clothes that say something to and about the person who wears them. Here are a few suggestions.

Beowulf (any edition).

Beowulf is said to be the oldest poem known in a modern European language. It is the story of a mythical Anglo-Saxon hero, but it is also a document about Christianity and the centuries before the Norman invasion.

Bhagavad-Gita (any edition).

This epic poem is one of the keys to understanding Hinduism and, through it, the culture of India.

Budge, E. A. Wallis. *Amulets and Talismans*. New York: Macmillan, 1970.

Budge was a scholar of ancient Egyptian and Middle Eastern antiquities. His book on sacred and magical symbols is one of the standard works in the field.

Bulfinch's Mythology (any edition).

The Bulfinch collection brings together many of the most important and familiar myths and legends of Western society, including ancient Greek and Roman stories, as well as those of the Norse and Germanic peoples, and the stories of the Age of Chivalry.

Campbell, Joseph. *The Masks of God*. Four volumes. New York: Viking Penguin, 1991.

Master mythologist Joseph Campbell examines the origins, place, and purpose of mythology in the past and present.

Frazer, James George. *The Golden Bough*. New York: Macmillan, 1985.

This may be the most complete single-volume study of the magical practices of early civilizations. Frazer's work explains the origins of many old customs and habits that persist in modern society.

Jung, Carl G., et al. *Man and His Symbols.* New York: Doubleday, 1969.

In this richly illustrated book, Jung and his associates applied his psychoanalytic theories to the study of symbols, both in image and in action.

Sams, Jamie, and David Carson. *Medicine Cards.* Santa Fe: Bear and Company, 1988.

Sams and Carson explain the meanings of totem animals from traditions all over North America. The accompanying card deck can be used for divination or as a study tool.

Sandars, Nancy K., trans., ed. *The Epic of Gilgamesh.* New York: Viking Penguin, 1972.

Gilgamesh was a demigod and king in Assyrian mythology. The Epic, which predates Homer by 1500 years, tells of his adventures and his search for eternal life.

Walker, Barbara G. *The Woman's Encyclopedia of Myths and Secrets.* San Francisco: Harper San Francisco, 1983.

Walker occasionally mistranslates Greek and Latin words, and sometimes fails to distinguish between a definition and a polemic, but this is nonetheless a valuable book for anyone interested in understanding women's roles in religion, mythology, and magic.

Wolkstein, Diane, and Samuel N. Kramer, trans., ed. *Inanna, Queen of Heaven and Earth.* New York: HarperCollins, 1983.

Inanna was the Sumarian counterpart of the goddess Ishtar. The star patterns so common in knitting come from symbols associated with the goddess-queen as the guarantor of fertility. Wolkstein and Kramer bring together stories and poems about Inanna translated from clay tablets nearly four thousand years old.

You might begin to think, after looking over the names of the publishers in this list, that we are fans of Dover books. In fact, we are, and have been for many years. Dover is a good source of inexpensive design and idea books for artists and craftspeople. Many of their titles are classics that would otherwise be difficult or impossible to find in print. Most of their books are assembled as "quality paperbacks" and will stand up to years of reading, thumbing, and being banged about in your workroom. Dover's Pictorial Archive Series has been especially valuable for us. Pictorial Archive books feature a minimum of text in favor of large, clear illustrations which artists may use with few copyright restrictions. Write to Dover Publications, 31 East Second Street, Mineola, New York 11501, for the Pictorial Archive catalog or a general catalog.

Sources

Here is a list of vendors who supply our tools and materials. We have been dealing with these folks for years and have always received good service. There are certainly other wonderful yarn mills and suppliers, but we know these well. All of these sources will deal with you mail order or will direct you to a source near you.

Cochineal Computer Knit Products, P.O. Box 4276, Encinitas, California 92024. (619) 942-1957. *Susan Lazear worked as a computer graphics artist and textile designer before setting up her own business to market computer knitting products. Cochineal's lead item is a software and hardware package called the Bit Knitter. The Bit Knitter's software and interface allow machine knitters to design patterns on their home computers and then download the patterns to their knitting machines. Hand knitters can use the Bit Knitter as well for design work, and to file and store patterns electronically. The software is well-designed and technical support is good. Susan keeps in touch with registered Bit Knitter users through a regular newsletter, so they always know about* new products and software modifications.

Crystal Palace Yarns, 3006 San Pablo Avenue, Berkeley, California 94702. (415) 548-9988. *Crystal Palace Yarns offers good quality and great colors in yarns ranging from handknitting weight to bulky. Crystal Palace also has bamboo knitting needles and other wonderful hard-to-find knitting supplies.*

Dharma Trading Company, P.O. Box 150916, San Rafael, California 94915. (800) 542-5227. *Dharma sells by mail order the Deka Fabric Paint that we've used to add color to Fair Isle. Deka Fabric Paint is waterbased, non-fading, non-stiffening, machine washable and dry cleanable, and nontoxic. The color is set permanently with a steam iron. Dharma also carries many lines of dyes, if you need to increase or improve the yarn colors you've got to work with. Its catalog includes many Dover books, especially the copyright-free design series, and other books of interest to textile arts people. It also offers many plain white, natural-fiber, ready-to-dye, ready-made garments. If you're dyeing up a pot of yarn,*

172

throw in a shirt or leggings to have something to match. Free catalog.

JaggerSpun, Water Street, Springvale, Maine 04083. (207) 324-4455. *JaggerSpun makes 100% wool yarns that glide through a standard-bed knitting machine, full luxuriously, and* don't scratch! *People who fuss that wool sweaters are hot and uncomfortable find these lightweight and gentle. Whoever is in charge of JaggerSpun's colors deserves a hug; they have a hundred colors in plain and heathered yarns that are a blessing to the Fair Isle fanatic. JaggerSpun's prices are very reasonable.*

Knitking, 1228 Crenshaw Boulevard, Los Angeles, California 90010. (213) 938-2077. *We have used Knitking knitting machines since the 1970s and have always been satisfied. Their mail-order desk is helpful and prompt. Their service department can often explain a repair to you over the phone, and if you can't fix it yourself, you can load your machine on a UPS truck and Knitking will repair it and send it back to you. Their reconditioned used machines are as good as new. If there is no satisfactory knitting machine dealer in your area, you can deal directly with Knitking in Los Angeles by phone and UPS.*

Silk City Fibers, 155 Oxford Street, Paterson, New Jersey 07522. (210) 942-1100. *Silk City Fibers has many different sorts of yarns, from 350 yards per pound (bulky handknit) to 46,000 yards per pound (cobweb). The 5/2 perle cotton knits easily on a standard-bed knitting machine, and comes in seventy-seven colors. The ribbing knits up springy, the colors are fast, the cotton is glossy, and the sweaters come out of the washer and dryer looking good.*

Three Feathers Pewter, 221 Jones Street, P.O. Box 232, Shreve, Ohio 44676. *David and Sharon Jones hand-cast pewter buttons. They've made many molds from unusual and beautiful antique buttons; they offer contemporary designs, too. Their mail-order service is quick and prices are very reasonable. Free catalog.*

Index

*This cape is made to wear
when dancing along the
web of the world.*

*It is based on the feathered serpent pattern (pages 54–55). One version was made
with serpents appliquéd as the hem, cuffs, and front and neck bands. The serpents
were yellow, blue, red, and green. (See appliqué, pages 22–23.)*